MY DEAR BISHOPS . . .

MY DEAR BISHOPS . . .

An Open Letter to
the American Catholic Bishops

or

The Hungry Sheep Look Up,
and Are Not Fed

David R. Carlin

ACM Books

To order additional copies of this book, contact:
Xlibris LLC
1-888-795-4274
www.Xlibris.com
Orders@Xlibris.com
123924

CONTENTS

for David, Josh, and Margaret

CHAPTER 1

Introduction

My Dear Bishops:

There are two famous statements you ought to post in your offices and consult at least once a day. One is a line from Milton's "Lycidas": "The hungry sheep look up, and are not fed." The other is something Harry Truman said about the presidency, but it applies equally to the episcopal office: "The buck stops here."

You are the shepherds of the Catholic flock, and for a generation and more—ever since the very heady days of Vatican II in Rome and the sexual revolution in the United States—you have done (I say this with all due respect, and only after long hesitation) a damned poor job of feeding your sheep. If the Catholic Church in the United States has gone into a serious decline in the intervening years—and who can doubt that it has?—I'm afraid you'll have to take the lion's share of blame. The buck stops with the bishop.

Please pardon me for this blunt commencement of my open letter. Normally I don't relish giving offense, especially to the bishops of my Church. Besides, it is not quite the thing for a Catholic layperson like myself to chide bishops, especially in public. Early in the second century St. Ignatius, the bishop of Antioch (St. Peter himself had been the first bishop of Antioch), in the course of his journey to the place of his martyrdom, wrote a series of letters to various churches reminding Christians of the importance of maintaining solidarity with their bishops. I fully agree with Ignatius. This habit of solidarity with bishops—and of course with the pope, the "bishop of bishops"—has been one of the great causes, under God, of the historical success of the Catholic Church. On the other hand, one of the great causes of the historical failures of the Church has been the prevalence from time to time of bishops who were not up the challenges presented by their social and cultural and political circumstances. The last half-century in the United States has been one of those times of inadequate episcopal leadership. It would be too much to say that in the Catholic Church *everything* depends on the quality of episcopal leadership. But it would not be far off the mark to say that *almost everything* depends on it.

I feel uncomfortable writing this letter, but it's a letter *somebody* had to write. So why not me?

Besides, I believe I can justify my writing of this critical letter with a citation from Thomas Aquinas. In the second part of the second part of his *Summa Theologica*, in article 5 of question 33, Thomas asks the question: "Whether a man is bound to correct his prelate [bishop]?" He answers by saying that "the fraternal correction which is an act of charity is within the competency of everyone in respect of any person towards whom he is bound by charity [and of course one is bound by charity to his bishop], provided there is something in that person which requires correction." Thomas adds however that "when a subject corrects his prelate, he ought to do so in a becoming manner, not with impudence and harshness, but with gentleness and respect." I pray, dear bishops, that you will find that this letter, though frank in its attempt to engage in two of the spiritual works of mercy, namely "reproving the sinner" and "instructing the ignorant," is gentle and respectful, not harsh and impudent.

Besides, I am not writing to reprove and instruct *my own* bishop, Thomas Tobin of Providence, who in my opinion is doing a fine job in his office. Indeed he might well serve as a model for many others.

Let me point out that I don't mean to blame each of you bishops *individually*. Some bishops—a minority—did a fine job during the worst years. And most of you were not even in office during the very worst years;

you became bishops only relatively recently. In short, many of you are not individually blameworthy, and some of you are even praiseworthy. (Please keep this in mind if you happen to read this letter and find that some parts of it irritate you. Say to yourself, "This irritating author is not speaking about *me*; he's speaking about all those other bishops.") But your *order*—the order of bishops—has been very much at fault. It is your order, not you personally, that I mean to blame. But since you belong to this order, you must shoulder blame. Once you're elevated to the rank of bishop you participate not only in the powers and benefits and glories of your order; you participate as well in its historical failures. You assume a burden of collective guilt—much as all Americans share in the collective guilt of slavery and the maltreatment of native Americans, even those among us whose families (like my own) didn't even reside in America during the centuries in which slavery existed or Indians were expelled from their native grounds.

Of course collective guilt would be a terribly unjust thing if applied in a formal-judicial way; that is, if persons were tried in court and sentenced to punishment because of crimes committed by their parents or brothers or cousins. But when applied in a moral-informal way, the idea of collective guilt makes a great deal of sense. It made good sense, for instance, when Republicans all over America were punished in the 1974 elections because a single man—a man who in addition to being president of the United States was the head of their party, Richard Nixon—had been caught in serious acts of misbehavior. In a similar way it makes sense to blame *all* Catholic bishops for the failures of *some* of them; and likewise it makes sense to hold *all* Catholic priests responsible for the sexual sins committed by *some* Catholic priests.[1] Holding bishops, priests, and Nixon-era Republicans collectively guilty gives

---

[1] It must be admitted, however, that the right to blame all priests or all bishops or all Catholics generally is a right that has often been abused in recent years by persons whose motive is not so much to prevent future sex abuse as it is to do permanent damage to the Catholic religion. The right has also been abused by comedians (e.g., Jay Leno) who wish to get a cheap laugh at the expense of the Catholic priesthood.

them a strong incentive to clean up their institutions so as to insure that the wrongdoing in question won't happen again.

But what are the failures I'm talking about? What do you bishops—or more exactly, the order of bishops—deserve to be blamed for? There are six great failures I have in mind

1. Clerical sex abuse

First and most obvious of course is the sex-abuse scandal that hit the headlines of the nation's newspapers in 2002 (beginning with the Boston Globe), where it remained day after day, month after month, during that year and beyond. The scandal wasn't simply that many priests had sexually exploited children and teenagers. Bad as this was, an equal or even greater scandal was that many bishops had "covered up" the abuse and facilitated it either by faulty action or by inaction. This terrible scandal is still grabbing headlines right up to the present day. Granted, the dreadful headlines we've been reading for years are not purely the result of sexual abuse and its episcopal cover-up. They are the result of sexual abuse *plus* the will of many secularists and semi-secularists[2] in the mainstream media to shame and degrade the Catholic Church. But if priests and bishops hadn't handed a sword to anti-Christian secularists, the latter wouldn't have been able to drive the sword into the body of the Church.

Why did you bishops do this? Why did you cover up these sins, these crimes? Let's review some of the answers to this question.

(1) One of these answers is that some bishops (probably no more than a small number) had themselves at some point in their careers either engaged in sexual exploitation of minors or had been strongly tempted to do so. And so, in order not to be hypocrites, they winked at a line of conduct they too had either engaged in or were strongly inclined to.

---

[2]   I'll explain at some length later in the book what I mean by "secularist" and "semi-secularist." For now it is enough to say that the words are roughly equivalent to "atheistic anti-Christian" and "semi-atheist anti-Christian."

(2) Another standard answer is you bishops were acting the way members of an "old boys club" normally act. That is, you had a mentality of "we priests have to stick together," and so you were extremely reluctant to turn a fellow-priest over to the cops. (Speaking of the police, by the way, this is often the way police themselves behave, deeply reluctant to turn in a fellow-officer who misbehaves.)

(3) Again, there was a widespread belief that the right kind of psychological treatment could "cure" men of their tendency to sexually exploit underage boys (and sometimes girls). And so you bishops took the advice of many psychiatrists and clinical psychologists: you sent offending priests away to treatment centers, and when they returned, now presumably "cured," you gave them another parish assignment. And in the new parish, of course, they resumed their career of sexual exploitation.

(4) Yet another answer is that you bishops covered up in order to protect the Church. You didn't want the world to know how badly many priests had behaved, not the world of Catholics and not the broader world of non-Catholics. You feared for the reputation of the Church. And you feared too for the finances of the Church—and there were two things to be afraid of here. For one, an awareness of the bad priests might lead Catholics to cut back on their contributions to the Church. For another, a barrage of law suits might follow. Of course, as we are often told about political cover-ups, "the cover-up is worse than the crime itself." Rarely or never has the truth of this maxim been more convincingly demonstrated than in the Catholic sex-abuse scandal.

But in fairness to you bishops, it must be acknowledged that you faced a genuine moral dilemma here. You had a duty to report the criminal priests to the law-enforcement authorities, true. At the same time you had a very serious duty to protect the Church from financial and reputational damage. The world at large, both Catholic and non-Catholic, believes that the former duty easily trumps the latter; it thinks you should have understood this almost immediately, and that your failure to understand it indicates either your stupidity or your wickedness or both. This is easy for a person who is not a Catholic bishop to say. For most non-bishops see the Catholic Church as being in a legal position similar to a private corporation, whether a for-profit corporation like General

Motors or a non-profit corporation like Princeton University; that is, they view the Church as, legally speaking, a creature of the state, operating with the permission of, and according to the rules of, the state. But that's not the way the Church sees itself, and that's not the way you, as a Catholic bishop, see the Church. You see the Church as a creature, not of the state, but of Jesus Christ; that is, as a creature of God. For the sake of peace, the Church complies with the laws of the state and pretends, so to speak, that it *is* a creature of the state. Normally in the United States there is no harm in this pretense, since the First Amendment of the US Constitution provides a virtually absolute guarantee of religious freedom. But you as a Catholic bishop don't see the Church as subordinate to the state. The Church stands on a quite different foundation. So far from being subordinate to the state, the Church is, if anything, superior to the state. And so when you were faced with the question presented by priestly sex abuse, "Is it my greater duty to report the crime or to protect the reputation and wealth of the Church?" the answer was far from obvious. The answer may seem obvious to the man or woman in the street, but it was far from obvious to a Catholic bishop whose *first* duty was to care for the well-being of the Church. In the last analysis, of course, the crimes should have been reported right away, for the cover-up did far more damage to the Church than immediate reporting could have done.

(5) Another answer: fear of *scandal*—in the strict moral theology sense of that word. That is, you bishops feared that news of the bad priestly behavior might lead some Catholics to lose their religious faith, thereby putting the eternal salvation of their souls in jeopardy. You saw it as your duty not to do anything to drive Catholics out of the Church, and not to do anything that would keep non-Catholics from entering it. This duty conflicted with your legal duty to report crimes to the police, and you couldn't comply with both duties at once; so you gave priority to the duty not to facilitate scandal.

(6) Further, there is another answer, one rarely or never taken note of, a reason that is not discreditable to one who "thinks with the mind of the Church"—although it will seem not just discreditable but absurd to one who thinks with the mind of the secular world. According to the Catholic idea, sin is the worst of all evils: worse than poverty, disease, mental depression,

imprisonment, public disgrace, being tortured, etc. In holding this idea Catholicism agrees with Plato and Socrates, who said that it is worse to commit injustice than to be the victim of injustice; and it disagrees with the world's prevailing morality, according to which immoral conduct is immoral because it harms the body, the psyche, the property, or the reputation of the victim of this conduct, not because it harms the soul of the perpetrator. Expressing this Catholic idea—this very "strange" Catholic idea—in melodramatic language, John Henry Newman once wrote:

> She [the Catholic Church] holds that it were better for sun and moon to drop from heaven, for the earth to fail, and for all the many millions who are upon it to die of starvation in extremest agony, so far as temporal affliction goes, than that one soul, I will not say, should be lost, but should commit one single venial sin, should tell one wilful untruth, though it harmed no one, or steal one poor farthing without excuse. (*Anglican Difficulties*, Christian Classics, Westminster MD, 1969; p. 240.)

Now if you were a bishop who had this idea—and if you're a Catholic bishop you *should* have this idea—then, when confronted with a report that one of your diocesan priests had sexually seduced a young child or a teenage boy (or girl), your reaction would be that the priest is more unfortunate than the child or youngster; for the priest has damaged his *immortal soul* with the triple sin of vow-breaking, unnatural sex, and seduction. The boy or girl, on the other hand, has at worst committed only one kind of sin, and probably not even that; and if the boy or girl has suffered some psychological damage, well, however bad that may be, at least it is not sin, the worst of all evils. And so you, the bishop who agreed with Newman and Plato, would quite naturally be more concerned with the priest than with the boy or girl. "I must help the priest, who has suffered more," you would say to yourself, "rather than the boy or girl, who has suffered less."

(7) Another not entirely discreditable reason is the following. Sometimes in life, indeed often in life, situations arise in which one has a conflict of duties

and one cannot fulfill both duties; so one must choose between two duties, and in choosing to fulfill the one duty, one is choosing to neglect the other.[3] Most of these conflicts involve relatively small matters. But sometimes you may be faced with extremely hard choices between duties. For instance, you were (let's say in the 1980s) a bishop who had become aware that one of your priests had been guilty of sexually molesting an underage boy. As a citizen you have a duty to report this crime the police authorities; but as a bishop you have an especially important duty to your diocesan priests, to whom you stand in a relationship like a father to a son. How many fathers would phone the police upon realizing that their sons had committed a crime, even a serious crime? Wouldn't that feel like a great sin against your child? And so it was with bishops: how could they, as good "fathers," report their "sons" to the cops? Now it is easy for the general public to say that such a conflict of duties is a no-brainer; it should be the easiest thing in the world for a bishop to see that his duty to obey the law takes precedence over his duty to protect his priests. This is easy to say if you are not a bishop; and it is especially easy to say if you belong, as many persons do, to the Christianity-hating section of the general public. But if you are a bishop—that is, a father to your priests—it is far from easy to say.

It will be pointed out—and pointed out very correctly—that bishops who covered up priestly wrongdoing and criminality did in fact *not* protect the Church. On the contrary, they did very grave damage to the Church. And so, even if their motives were not entirely discreditable, their judgments and actions were faulty, extremely faulty. Catholics nowadays, decades after the vast majority of molestations took place (very few have taken place in recent decades), often complain when the media, e.g., the New York Times, keep

---

[3]   For a wonderfully entertaining example of this, see the novel by the Catholic author Graham Greene, *The Heart of the Matter*, where the hero (by the name of Scobie) has to choose between his wife and his adulterous girlfriend. He doesn't want to hurt either one; he pities them both. And so he resolves the dilemma by committing suicide. The author, without giving anything like a general approval of suicide, suggests that Scobie was making a Christ-like choice: as Jesus voluntarily died for love of mankind, so Scobie voluntarily died for love of his wife and his girlfriend.

running stories about priestly molestations and episcopal cover-ups. "This is ancient history," many Catholics say. "We have aired our dirty laundry, we have repented for our sins, we have taken effective steps to make sure this doesn't happen in the future. Bad as many of our priests were decades ago, Catholic priests today are far more likely to abstain from sexual molestation than are other men who work closely with children, e.g., public school teachers and Protestant ministers. And yet the mainstream media keep bashing the Catholic Church, paying hardly any attention to others agencies that may be offending in similar ways. This reflects a strong anti-Catholic bias. It is not fair." True enough: it is not fair, and it certainly does reflect an anti-Catholic bias. And this is true as well for persons who today, centuries after the events, still bash the Church for the Galileo affair and the Spanish Inquisition and the Crusades. If somebody, including the New York Times, has an anti-Catholic bias, the passage of decades and even of centuries will not deter him or them from using old scandals to defame the Church. The Galileo scandal will not soon disappear, and neither will the priestly sex-abuse scandal. Never mind fairness. There will be no reason for surprise if centuries from now Catholic priests are still stereotyped as sexual molesters. And it was you bishops—whatever some of your not-entirely-discreditable intentions may have been—who handed this weapon to the enemies of the Church just as earlier the Galileo tribunal handed a similar weapon to those enemies

2. Clerical homosexuality

It has been customary for the secular press to call these abusive priests "pedophiles" and to speak of their crime as "pedophilia." Properly speaking, however, these are not the correct words, since pedophilia, correctly defined, is a sexual interest in pre-pubescent children; and the great majority of the abuse covered up by bishops had, not pre-pubescent children as its target, but adolescents. And of adolescents, not teenage girls, but teenage boys[4] were its chief target. The correct English word for this kind of sexual interest—namely, an adult male lusting for the body of a teenage male who has already reached the age of puberty—is "homophilia" or "homosexuality."[5]

For anyone who has kept up with the depressing journalistic news of the sex-abuse scandal, or read about[6] or listened to anecdotal evidence about life in Catholic seminaries since the 1960s, it has been impossible to avoid the inference that seminaries and the priesthood abounded with homosexuals[7] beginning in the 1960s. And seminaries and the priesthood abounded not just with those who exploited, or would sooner or later exploit, teenage boys but also with those who carried on fully consensual relations with adult men. How could you bishops not have known this? How could you have been so blind? And how, knowing it, could you have let it slide? How could you have been so unrealistic as to imagine that a homosexual-intensive priesthood would not eventually lead to big trouble—especially in an era in which sexual liberation and moral skepticism were abounding in the general culture of America?

Of course some bishops (probably not many) were themselves homosexuals[8] who didn't want to be hypocritical by cracking down on gays in

---

[4] According to the report commissioned by the United States Conference of Catholic Bishops, popularly known as the John Jay Report, in which criminologists from John Jay College analyzed priestly sexual abuse, 81 percent of the abuse had male victims, 19 percent female.

[5] It can also be called *ephebophilia*, a sexual interest in boys or girls who have reached puberty but have not yet reached adulthood. Ephebophilia comes in two varieties, homosexual and heterosexual. The great majority of the priestly sex abuse was homosexual ephebophilia.

[6] Michael Rose's book, *Goodbye, Good Men,* is more anecdotal than scientific or comprehensive. Nonetheless its many anecdotes, when combined with press reports and the John Jay Report, paint a very convincing picture.

[7] When I say "homosexuals" here, I don't mean chaste men who happened to have a same-sex orientation; I mean men who were either sexually active or favorably disposed to being sexually active.

[8] The best-known instance of a homosexual bishop is Rembert Weakland, for many years the Archbishop of Milwaukee. Prior to his fall, it is worth noting, Weakland was a tremendous favorite among liberal/progressive Catholics.

the seminary or priesthood. Or they feared that they could become victims of blackmail if they decided to crack down. Or they weren't just *potential* victims of blackmail but actual victims—their gay priests told them: "If you punish or restrict me, I'll expose you." Most bishops, however, were simply naive, blind either to the fact of widespread clerical homosexuality or to the probable consequences of it. Being naive can sometimes be a charming characteristic—in young children, for example. But it is definitely *not* charming in bishops. Rather, it is a very grave fault. A bishop is a leader of men and women, and a leader needs to have a realistic understanding both of the world in general and of his followers in particular. The buck stops with the bishop. Your failure to deal with homosexuality—and not just homosexual inclinations, which were troublesome enough, but homosexual conduct—in seminaries and in the priesthood was a dreadful thing; one might almost say a diabolical thing. It had much to do—maybe everything to do—with the ensuring "pedophilia" scandal.

3. Abortion

But tolerating and covering up clerical homosexuality and sex abuse were not the only failings of you bishops, and not even the worst. You failed on abortion as well. It is true that when the United States Supreme Court issued its controversial *Roe v. Wade* ruling in January of 1973, striking down virtually every abortion-restriction law in the land, many Catholic bishops immediately did valiant work at mobilizing anti-abortion sentiment and political activity. But before long these efforts, which were led by an older generation of Catholic bishops, waned, and Catholic opposition to abortion, apart from an opposition that was not much more than pro forma, largely fizzled out. If the prolife cause is alive and well in the United States today—and it is very much alive and well—this is mainly because of Evangelical Protestants. Catholics play no more than a minor role. Just the opposite, in fact. If Catholics play any truly significant role in the abortion controversy, it is on the pro-abortion side. Today states with the highest percentage of Catholics in their population—for instance, Massachusetts, Rhode Island, Connecticut, New York, New Jersey—lead the way in sending pro-abortion senators and representatives to Washington. Politically speaking, the pro-abortion force in the United States is largely an alliance between a leadership group of atheists, agnostics, and their liberal[9] Christian fellow-travelers,[10] plus a follower group of Catholic voters.

The pro-abortion movement—and this is a point that you bishops, hard though it is to believe, don't seem to get—has not been simply a movement *in favor of* abortion; it has been a movement *against* Christianity in general and against Catholicism in particular.[11] The anti-Christianity syllogism goes something like this:

- If Christianity, which teaches that abortion is wrong, is a true religion, then abortion is wrong.
- But abortion is *not* wrong.
- Therefore Christianity is a false religion.

This implicit attack on Christianity isn't the product of the abortion movement only. It is the entire "sexual revolution" (SR) that has been attacking Christianity, with the abortion movement being only one section—one prominent, powerful, and well-organized section—of the SR. I'll have more to say about this in a later chapter, but for now let me simply remind you bishops of something you must know (how could you possibly not know it?), yet it

---

9   Throughout the book I'll be using the word "liberal" (with negative connotation) to label those "Christians" who have, in effect, defected from traditional Christianity in an attempt to create an incoherent religion situated approximately halfway between Christianity and outright anti-Christianity. I regret having to use the word "liberal," since it's a fine old word with many fine associations, e.g., "liberal arts" and "liberal democracy." But what can I do? For more than a century the adjective "liberal" has been attached to the kind of incoherent religion I have in mind. It's too late now to begin calling it something else.

10 Below I'll often have more to say about this important and powerful alliance between secularists and liberal Christians.

11 The same is true of the gay movement: it is not simply a movement in favor of homosexuals and homosexuality; it is a movement *against* Christianity.

somehow drops out of your mind when you confront the contemporary culture of the United States. I refer to the tremendous emphasis on chastity—most people today would say the neurotic *over*-emphasis—that has always been characteristic of traditional Christianity, above all of Catholic Christianity. Your religion has always insisted on a strict, indeed a super-strict, sexual ethic: no sex outside of marriage; inside marriage no contraception and no "unnatural" sex; no divorce-and-remarriage; no homosexuality, not even for persons with a stable homosexual orientation; no masturbation; no pornography; and so on. Moreover, other things being equal, a life of consecrated celibacy and virginity has always been considered by Catholicism to be superior even to a life of marital chastity. This superiority largely explains why ordination to the priesthood has been legally confined, at least for the past thousand years or so, to those who are unmarried: even morally licit married sex, it seems to have been felt, would "sully" the man who in the Eucharist turns bread and wine into the body and blood of Christ. Now this extreme emphasis on chastity and virginity has never been a merely incidental feature of Catholicism. It has always been very near the ethical center of the religion; it is part of what may be called the *Catholic core*. But what has been the attitude of the SR toward the Catholic idea of chastity? From the SR point of view, the Catholic idea of chastity is *complete nonsense*. In other words, something at the core of Catholicism is mere foolishness. But if *this* is nonsense, then Catholicism as a whole is nonsense. To imagine that you can have Catholicism without a strong emphasis on chastity is something like imagining that you can have a circle that isn't round. A Catholicism that is compatible with the SR (the kind of Catholicism that many liberal/progressive Catholics seem to hope for) is in effect a contradiction in terms; there is no such thing, nor can there be.

The SR, then, has been from the beginning, and still is, an attack on Catholicism—and I may add, an extremely effective attack. I don't mean, however, that it has been a *conscious and deliberate* attack; for some pro-SR people it is that kind of attack, but not for most. I don't suppose, for instance, that there is an SR politburo that meets every Monday morning over coffee and Danish to plot the week's strategy for the destruction of Catholicism. No, it is mainly a de facto attack. If somebody gives you food laced with toxic chemicals, he is attacking your life, even if his purpose in giving you the poison was not to injure you but merely to enhance the flavor of your meal.

I should add that this SR attack on Catholicism is also an attack on conservative Protestantism, indeed on all forms of old-fashioned Christianity. Protestantism has never laid so strong an emphasis on chastity and sexual abstinence as has Catholicism. No matter in what country or region the Reformation prevailed during the 16th century, the reformers immediately did away with monasteries, nunneries, and a celibate priesthood. Nonetheless traditional Protestantism retained a strong emphasis on chastity. It insisted on premarital virginity and marital fidelity; and while in theory it permitted divorce (on account of adultery), in practice it strongly discouraged divorce, which was almost as rare in Protestant as in Catholic countries. The strict sexual ethic of Puritanism was a Protestant thing, as was the strict middle-class sexual ethic of the Victorian Age. It is only in the 20th century, and especially in the last third of that century, that American Protestantism adopted a much more relaxed sexual ethic—and it is liberal Protestantism alone, not conservative (Evangelical and Pentecostal) Protestantism, that has become sexually more permissive. Conservative Protestantism remains as attached as ever to the ideal of chastity.[12]

As you bishops know, just as everybody knows, the pro-abortion movement has been an essential ingredient of the SR—for how can we have what the SR demands, namely a cultural regime of tremendous sexual freedom, if we don't have abortion available to take care of "mistakes"? Regardless, then, of whether you look at the fight for abortion rights all by itself, or look at it as an essential ingredient of the SR, it has been a de facto struggle against Catholicism (and all traditional Christianity). And so the failure of American Catholicism to fight effectively against abortion has been a failure to fight

---

[12]   It is needless to point out that the Catholic and Protestant high valuation of chastity does not mean that Catholics and Protestants have always lived perfectly chaste lives. No, for it is possible for a person honestly to believe that chastity is a good thing without himself/herself being especially chaste. That chastity is a great virtue is one teaching of Christianity; that all men and women are sinners is another.

against attacks on itself; a failure to engage in self-defense. The blame for this failure rests, not just with you bishops, but with Catholic priests and nuns[13] and lay persons generally. But the failure rests above all with you bishops. You are the captain of the team, the shepherd of the flock. You failed to mobilize your people. Granted, this would not have been easy work. But this doesn't change the fact that you bishops didn't get the job done. As President Truman said: "The buck stops here." When things go wrong, the leader at the top of the organizational pyramid has to take the blame. Baseball managers get blamed when the team has a bad season. The Catholic Church in the United States has had a long series of bad seasons. You bishops, you managers of the "team" that is the Catholic Church in the United States, have to take the blame.

Before abandoning the subject of abortion (which I'm doing only for a short while, since I'll have a lot more to say about this later in the book), let me say a word about "the hungry sheep" who "look up and are not fed." Anybody even moderately familiar with the Catholic wing of the prolife movement soon becomes aware of a dissatisfaction with bishops that has been widespread among Catholic members of that movement. They feel themselves to be fighting in defense not just of a great moral principle but of a great *Catholic* moral principle. They feel moreover that in fighting for this they are fighting in defense of their Catholic religion. And they are right. They intuitively understand what I have discursively argued for above, namely, that the pro-abortion movement is de facto (and ipso facto) an anti-Catholic movement. Now with very few exceptions these prolife Catholics are not "lunatic fringe" types, not the kind of people who may be described as "more Catholic than the pope." No, they are ordinary Catholics—mainly women, it is worth noting—who happen to take their religion and its teachings seriously. As such, they see themselves as doing exactly the kind of work that their bishops would like them to do. Why, then, don't they get more support from their bishops? Why have most bishops, they wonder, been so weak in their

---

[13] Since the 1970s American nuns—that is, the few of them who did not abandon the convent—have been strongly influenced by the feminist movement, which has been among other things a pro-abortion movement. Hence many nuns (e.g., the notorious Sr. Simone Campbell) have tended to be "soft" on abortion.

resistance to the anti-Catholic, anti-Christian abortion movement? Why have bishops been more worried about giving offense to "dissident" Catholics than about giving offense to true-blue Catholics?

4. Generic Christianity

Yet—hard though this is to believe—there is something *even worse* than your failures on clerical homosexuality and abortion, and this "something worse" underlies the other failures. Among American Catholics, the Catholic faith has come to be seriously watered down in the last generation or so. This is the phenomenon often called "a la carte Catholicism" or "cafeteria Catholicism" or "pick-and-choose Catholicism." Many American Catholics, probably most, have decided that it is perfectly possible to be a Catholic without accepting the full teaching of the Catholic Church, indeed while positively rejecting certain teachings of the Church. According to this view, you can remain a Catholic in good standing even though you disagree with the Church on one or more of the following: birth control, premarital sex, remarriage-after-divorce, abortion, homosexuality, the Virgin Birth, the Incarnation, the Trinity, the Atonement, the Resurrection, the Real Presence in the Eucharist, the priestly ordination of women—the list goes on and on and on. Great numbers of Catholics have in effect silently dropped the Catholic religion and adopted an alternative religion. What's the name of this alternative? Call it *Generic Christianity*. Instead of the ancient and very complex creed of Catholicism, Generic Christianity has a modern, streamlined creed consisting of three articles: (1) God loves us all;[14] (2) Jesus our brother was a good and wise man who taught, both by example and by precept, many first-class ethical ideals; and (3) we must love our neighbors.

---

[14] The phrase "just as we are" is often added to this assurance that God loves us all. In other words, God, who is apparently as tolerant as the most liberal of American liberals, is not especially troubled by the fact that a person may be living in a state of habitual sin. But if there is nothing especially wrong with sin, then Catholicism becomes nonsense. For if sin is not a major issue, why did Jesus Christ take the trouble to die for our sins?

This is a very nice creed—but is it a *Catholic* creed? No, of course not. Thus we have in America (and not just in America) the absurd situation that many people who are counted as Catholics positively disbelieve in Catholicism. In fact the 3-article creed of Generic Christianity is a creed not very far removed from the belief system of decent atheists and agnostics. They too hold that we should love our neighbors; that is to say, we should do no harm to our fellow human beings, and we should help them when they are in need—by voting, for example, for political candidates who believe in helping the poor, promoting world peace, opposing the death penalty, defending abortion rights, supporting same-sex marriage, etc. And these decent atheists and agnostics often admire Jesus. They do not, of course, regard Jesus as divine or as being literally heaven-sent, but they think he was a fine man who taught some first-class ethical ideals. And they are convinced—or at least they *pretend* to be convinced when debating moral questions with moral conservatives—that were Jesus on earth today he would vote for the same candidates they vote for; in other words, Jesus would be a political liberal, a reliable Democratic voter. And so they hold two-thirds of the creed of Generic Christianity. If you are an orthodox Catholic believer you are *many* steps removed from being an atheist or agnostic: to make the transition from belief to unbelief you'd have to drop, as a minimum, your belief in Divine Revelation, your belief in the articles of the Nicene Creed, your belief that the Bible is the inspired word of God, your belief that the Catholic Church headed by the pope is the divinely authorized preserver and interpreter of Divine Revelation, plus a dozen other beliefs that the Church and the Bible teach. But if you're Generic Christian you have to drop only one thing to pass to the status of atheist or agnostic, namely your belief in God. And if you are a Generic Christian it is probable that your belief in God is no more than a half-belief; so it's really only a half-step from Generic Christianity to outright unbelief. If I am correct, then, in assuming that many, perhaps even most, American Catholics (that is, Americans who *call* themselves Catholic) are actually believers, not in Catholicism, but in Generic Christianity, then such Catholics are on the verge of crossing the line to outright unbelief. If they don't cross the line themselves, there is a great likelihood that their children or grandchildren will cross the line; for a "thin" religion like Generic Christianity cannot easily be transmitted to the younger generations in the family.

The creed of Generic Christianity was created during the first half of the 20th century by liberal Protestants of an "ecumenical" frame of mind. With the goal of Christian unity in mind, they wanted to break down the walls that separated one denomination from another; and a very effective way of doing this, they supposed, was to toss overboard, or at least strongly de-emphasize, those points of doctrine that distinguish one Christian denomination from another. Something like the creed outlined above seemed to them to constitute basic or essential Christianity, a least-common-denominator creed that would allow all Christians, even those with a temperamental aversion to dogma, to sit at the same table. I say "something like" that creed, since this pan-Protestant creed was a "thicker" creed in the first half of the 20th century; for in those days it included a consensus on morality, especially sexual morality. In the second half of the century that moral consensus collapsed as liberal Protestantism more and more embraced the sexual revolution and increasingly gave its approval to fornication, abortion, homosexuality, and same-sex marriage. When in the 1960s Catholics at long last threw down the walls of their "ghetto" and entered the mainstream of American social-cultural life, they quite naturally embraced the Generic Christianity of their liberal Protestant neighbors; for in those days liberal Protestantism was the culturally dominant worldview in the United States.[15]

There is, I grant, much that can be said in favor of this religion of Generic Christianity. Those who embrace it have no motive for fighting one another over religious issues; and eliminating motives for fighting is a positive thing in a society like ours; that is, a society whose principal business is producing goods and services that can be bought and sold. Further, Generic Christianity has the potential of being good for political peace; for if all Americans were to become Generic Christians there would be no religion-related political issues to fight about. But there's the rub. All Americans have *not* become Generic

---

[15] This is no longer true. Today secularism is the dominant worldview in the United States. On this, more later.

Christians, and it is unlikely that all of us will become Generic Christians in the remotely foreseeable future. Instead the rise of Generic Christianity has created a great social-cultural divide in America: on one side the Generic Christians (along with their atheistic and agnostic cousins); on the other, conservative or old-fashioned believers in dogmatic religion—orthodox Catholics, Evangelical and Pentecostal Protestants, Eastern Orthodox believers—who refuse to embrace the watered-down creed of Generic Christianity.[16]

I'll grant, as I said, that there is something to be said in favor of Generic Christianity—but one thing that cannot be said is that it is Catholicism, or even close to Catholicism. "Catholics" who embrace it are quite simply not Catholic, at least not if Catholicism is defined, as it has been defined since the early days of the Christian religion, in terms of orthodox belief. The Catholicism held by many American Catholics today, perhaps even by most of them, is a very watered-down Catholicism. It is a not-really-Catholic Catholicism.

Given that the real religion of many of today's American Catholics is Generic Christianity, can anyone be surprised that very few Catholic young persons become priests or nuns, that Sunday church attendance is way down, that Catholics are not awfully successful at transmitting their religion to their children, that almost no Catholics believe contraception to be sinful, or that Catholics engage in fornication and unmarried cohabitation and abortion at about the same rates as everybody else? Can anyone be surprised that homosexuals have invaded the priesthood or that Catholics are reliable supporters of pro-abortion politicians? In short, who can be surprised that the Catholic religion in the United States has undergone a great decline and fall during the last generation or two?[17] This great transformation—from orthodox Catholicism to Generic Christianity—has taken place during the

---

[16]   In this division between liberal and traditional Christians, persons belonging to the Church of Latter-Day Saints (Mormons) often find themselves on the same side as the traditionalists, even though Mormonism is far from being a traditional form of Christianity. But if it is not traditional, it is not liberal or modernistic either. And in questions of morality, Mormonism *is* traditional.

[17]   For a more detailed account of this decline, see my book *The Decline and Fall of the Catholic Church in America* (Sophia Institute Press, 2003).

last 40 or 50 years. Let me repeat myself: the people who must take the principal blame for this are those who sit (often they sit on their hands) at the top of the organizational pyramid, namely you bishops. The buck stops with you.

5. The spread of same-sex marriage

The geographical section of the United States in which moral liberals, that is, atheists and agnostics and their liberal Christian fellow-travelers, have been most successful in advancing the cause of same-sex marriage (SSM) has been the Northeast—precisely the section of the country most densely populated with Catholics (by Catholics here I mean people who call themselves Catholic, even though they may in fact be no more than Generic Christians). You bishops, in other words, have been defeated in your own backyards again and again by gay activists and their liberal allies. When I say "you" have been defeated, I mean that Catholicism has been defeated; for if homosexuality is morally licit, then (to repeat the syllogism I offered above regarding abortion) Catholicism is a false religion, since Catholicism has always taught that homosexual behavior is morally illicit, very seriously morally illicit: not a venial sin but a mortal sin, and not a minor mortal sin but a major mortal sin. And when a state enacts a same-sex marriage law, the state is declaring in effect that homosexual conduct is morally licit and that Catholic morality is nonsense. You bishops have been defeated again and again even though you had a huge population of Catholic voters you could have called upon, could have mobilized—or at least tried to mobilize. But you left these masses non-mobilized, you left them passive and apathetic, while you were being defeated by small numbers of smart, well-organized, technologically savvy anti-Christian activists and fanatics. Why weren't you smart and well-organized too? It is as if your large army fought with cavalry and swords against a much smaller enemy equipped with tanks and machine guns. Better still, while the enemy was rolling its tanks across the landscape of your dioceses, your cavalry was still in the barn, munching hay.

I realize of course that your enemies are formidable. They control the mainstream media in the Northeast (think of the Boston Globe and New York Times, for instance) just as they generally control the mainstream media nationwide. And so for many years the people of your region have been receiving a steady stream of pro-SSM propaganda. Nationwide the campaign in support of SSM received a tremendous boost in 2012 when the President of the United States announced that he too was in favor of SSM; his "evolution" on this topic was finally complete. Of course, as everybody but those who are hopelessly naïve realized well before the announcement, Mr. Obama had been in favor of SSM for years; no evolution was needed. His declaration in 2008 that he was opposed to SSM was nothing more than a convenient political lie. He was simply waiting for an opportune moment to announce his support for SSM. In 2008 the moment was not yet, in his astute political judgment, ripe. But by mid-2012 the moment of ripeness had arrived. Ironically, it was Obama's Catholic Vice-President, Joe Biden, who set the table for Obama's announcement when Biden himself, a few days earlier, announced his own support for SSM on a Sunday morning talk show. In any case, both at the national level and at the regional level the propaganda campaign in favor of SSM has been going on for many years, and has been very effective. An especially effective element of that propaganda was the argument that SSM was inevitable. Public opposition to SSM was concentrated, according to public opinion polls, among older Americans; by contrast, younger persons were lopsidedly in support of SSM. And of course older people are dying off, which means that control of society shifts from them to younger generations; and if the younger generations don't have a radical change of mind as they grow older, they will approve of, and enact, laws allowing SSM. So the argument in favor of the inevitability of SSM is a very plausible argument.

This inevitability argument is sometimes expressed in the form of "being on the right side of history"—the idea here being that the newer thing, whatever it may happen to be, is an improvement on the older thing. And so if—like the pope and the bishops and the Catholic religion—you oppose SSM, you are on the *wrong side* of history. Now this idea that the newer is always better than the older is generally true with regard to science and technology, but it is fallacious when applied to morality and religion and politics. But most people don't notice the fallacy, for we Americans are so in love with "progress" that we are apt to consider all change to be genuine progress. And thus we often find idealistic Americans claiming that they wish to be "change agents," by which they mean that they hope to make the world better. They forget that Hitler and Lenin, not to mention Genghis Khan and Attila the Hun, were change agents. They assume that all "change" is change for the better. And thus candidate Obama in 2008 was able to use the one-word slogan "Change," and everybody read that to mean "change for the better." In any case, talk about inevitability and being on the right side of history has been, and continues to be, enormously effective in the great propaganda campaign in support of SSM. So you bishops have had your work cut out for you.

Nonetheless you could have prevailed if you had succeeded in mobilizing your Catholic masses. I realize of course that you made some attempts to do this. You made pronouncements against SSM; but by and large these were ineffectual. Spectacularly ineffectual. Why were they so ineffectual? There are, I suggest, three main reasons.

The first of these is the general decline over the past half-century of the teaching authority—which includes, by implication, the political authority—of Catholic bishops. There are many reasons for this, some of them outlined in the earlier sections of this chapter, e.g., the rise of Generic Christianity among Catholics, and the sex-abuse scandal. There was a time when American Catholics were generally responsive to the word of their bishops. That time has long since passed.

Second, you bishops had very little support from your parish priests in your campaign against SSM. At a minimum you needed your priests, when delivering homilies, to tell their parishioners that the Catholic Church—*their* Church—teaches and has always taught that homosexual behavior is morally wrong, is unnatural and sinful; and that therefore they (the parishioners) have a duty as citizens to oppose enactment of SSM laws, which in effect endorse unnatural behavior. Very few priests actually did this. It is a rare Catholic priest in America who sermonizes on any sex-related topic. When is the last time a Catholic parishioner heard a sermon denouncing contraception or fornication or even abortion? How many parishioners have ever heard a sermon reminding them that homosexual behavior is a sin? And if parish priests were silent, declining to reinforce the message of the bishop about homosexuality and SSM, how could the bishop's message be effectual? Worse, the silence of the parish priest undercuts the bishop's message. It is as if the silent priest is by implication telling his parishioners, "You don't really have to take the bishop seriously on this matter."

There are three categories of priests who gave their bishops little or no support in the struggle against SSM—and these three categories, it should be noted, to a great extent overlap one another. (1) Older priests from the Vatican II era who are still believers in "the spirit of Vatican II." These priests, who still after all these decades think of themselves as "progressives," are as a matter of principle, or at least of deeply ingrained habit, always reluctant to oppose the "wisdom" the secular world has to offer; and thus, while they don't go so far as to endorse fornication or abortion or homosexuality, they are unwilling to stand in the pulpit and denounce them. These are the same priests who, influenced by feminism (an important element of the "wisdom" of the secular world), are sure that the Catholic Church will eventually, like the churches of the Anglican Communion, ordain women as priests and bishops. And these are the priests who, out of respect for feminist sensibilities, "improve" some words of the Creed, changing them from "and became man" to "and became one of us." (2) Those priests who don't want to give offense to their parishioners by denouncing from the pulpit certain sins that are looked on with approval by some of their parishioners. If you denounce abortion you'll offend parishioners who have had abortions or whose family members have had abortions; ditto for denunciations of homosexuality; and ditto for denunciations of fornication and unmarried cohabitation. Did the Apostle Paul denounce behavior of this kind? Yes. But Paul, lucky fellow that he was, didn't have the great burden and responsibility of leading an American parish in the modern world. If you offend these parishioners with your denunciations, they may turn away from Catholicism. This will reduce the parish revenue; but that's a small point. The big point is that driving these people away from the Church will place their immortal souls in jeopardy. What good pastor would wish to do that? And so these priests preach a watered-down version of Catholicism, a version that pretty much corresponds to the Generic Christianity I spoke of earlier; that is, a Christianity that gives offense to nobody because it doesn't disapprove of any behavior that parishioners approve of. This is a species of Christianity whose morality can be pretty much summed up as, "Let's all be nice to one another." (3) Those priests who simply have no idea of what kind of world they are living in. They are sociologically and historically naïve. They have noticed that not as many people come to church as used to attend in the old days; and they have also noticed that vocations to the priesthood or the convent are way down from what they were sixty years ago; and they know (not from the confessional, for nobody goes to confession anymore) from watching TV that the nation abounds in sexual sin. But these naïve priests haven't been able to put 2 plus 2 together. It hasn't dawned on them that a great anti-Christianity cultural crusade has been going on in America for decades now, led by atheistic anti-Christians and aided and abetted by liberal Christians. They don't realize that Catholicism, if it is not to shrink to something small and insignificant in America, had better fight back.

In the old days, before there was such a thing as a "priest shortage," a bishop could compel parish priests to co-operate with him by letting them understand that there is a price to pay for non-co-operation. For one thing, priests who failed to co-operate would never become pastors of a parish; instead they would remain forever mere assistant pastors. Worse still, as assistant pastors they'd be assigned to a parish in the boondocks or in the slums, where they would have to work under the supervision of a pastor who was a grouchy alcoholic. And the bishop would not actually have to say this to any priest in so many words; every priest in the diocese would understand the system; they would have first learned about it by hearing rumors and anecdotes during their apprenticeship in the seminary. But in our priest-shortage days a bishop can no longer do this. In the old days there were many more priests in a diocese than there were parishes; now many dioceses have more parishes than priests. If priests today obey their bishop, it is not out of fear, but out of respect for his position; and as every armed police officer knows, respect plus fear wins more obedience than respect alone.

Third, you bishops don't seem to understand what your anti-Christianity opponents understand very well, namely, that we Americans are living in the midst of a revolution in communications technology: we are living in an age of emails, Facebook, Twitter, and so on and so forth. Pro-SSM enthusiasts wield these new weapons with great skill. You bishops lag far, far behind. *They* mobilize and motivate their supporters with daily—sometimes hourly—direct messages using these new technologies. *You* rely on old means of communication. You issue an occasional press release via the secular press; you make statements in your diocesan newspapers (which hardly anybody reads); you hope (mostly this is a vain hope) that your parish priests will convey your message to their parishioners; and on very rare occasions you issue a pastoral letter. In other words, when it comes to communicating with your flock, you are a day late and a dollar short. You are stuck in the middle of the 20th century, if not in the middle of the 12th century, while your deadly foes are operating in the second decade of the 21st century.

An early sign of this episcopal incapacity was the failure of the US Conference of Catholic Bishops (in those days called the National Conference of Catholic Bishops) to create a national Catholic TV channel in the days when cable TV was first rapidly expanding. You didn't have to be a genius to understand that cable TV had a great future and that there would be room for a Catholic channel. But the bishops missed the train. Instead the Catholic channel (EWTN) was created by a hitherto obscure nun from Alabama, Mother Angelica. In saying this I don't mean to speak slightingly of Mother Angelica. Far from it. I regard her as one of the great figures in American Catholic history. But the opening that she saw and seized upon, you bishops could have—*should* have—seen and seized upon. That you did not do so was an indication of your incapacity to fight the good fight in a world of modern communications technology. (On the other hand, you bishops are so poor at this kind of thing that if you *had* pre-empted Mother Angelica, your product might well have been awful. Hers is awful some of the time. Yours might have been awful all of the time. Maybe it's just as well she beat you to it.)

And this communications incapacity continued into the age of the Internet. It is, I submit, nothing less than a scandal that the USCCB has failed to construct a vast data base of the phone numbers and email addresses of all (or nearly all) church-going Catholics in the United States. This would allow bishops to send mass emails to their people or to make mass phone calls to them. If such a data base had existed, bishops could have utilized it to urge their Catholic flocks to communicate with their state legislators in order to stop SSM legislation. I don't mean to say that the ordinary use of such a communications system—a system that would allow any bishop to communicate instantaneously with almost all the church-going Catholics in his diocese—would be to influence legislators. Normally the system would be used for preaching the Gospel, that is, for carrying out the "Great Commission" that Jesus gave to his apostles (Matthew 27:19-20). Only on very special occasions would there be a need to activate the system to deal with legislative matters. But it is certainly a "special occasion" when an American state considers altering the immemorial definition of marriage, thereby giving its sanction to behavior that the ancient Jewish-Christian religious-moral tradition has always considered unnatural and gravely sinful, a great offense against God, an abomination.

It might be objected that to allow a bishop to go "over the heads" of his parish priests in this way would be a violation of the great Catholic principle of subsidiarity, according to which higher-level institutions and organizations should not usurp the legitimate functions of lower-level institutions and organizations; only when, says the principle of subsidiarity, a task cannot be achieved, or at least not well-achieved, at a lower level should a higher-level organization step in and perform that task. And thus, it may be argued, it would be wrong for a bishop to do what falls within the province of parish priests. But when it comes to the "culture war" and the defense of Catholicism against its enemies, parish priests are by and large *not* performing their tasks well. And even if they were, a bishop does not usurp the function of parish priests when he sends an email to Catholics in his diocese any more than he usurps that function when he issues a pastoral letter or when he writes an opinion essay in his diocesan newspaper; or any more than the pope usurps the function of bishops when the pope issues an encyclical letter.

6. The worst thing of all: the fundamental failure

You bishops, with an occasional and praiseworthy exception here and there, have failed to take appropriate and effective action regarding the five above items (sex abuse, homosexuals invading the priesthood, abortion, Generic Catholicism, and the push for SSM) because you have failed to understand the most important thing of all—that the atheists and near-atheists of America have for a generation or more been conducting a very effective cultural "crusade" against Christianity, especially Christianity in its old-fashioned forms, and above all Christianity in its Catholic form. Or if you have perhaps understood this, you have failed to act on your understanding; at least you have failed to act with any significant degree of effectiveness.

As I will try to show in later chapters of this book, atheism, after having been quiet and ineffectual in America for centuries, has emerged as a powerful cultural and political force in recent decades. And the aim, or at least the clear tendency, of this cultural-political force has been to destroy traditional Christianity and the code of morality associated with it, most conspicuously the code of sexual morality. In an attempt to be more precise, I should perhaps speak of an "anti-Christianity coalition," a coalition made up of three sections: (1) outright atheists; (2) agnostics who are virtually atheistic; and (3) liberal Christians (and Jews) who, though rejecting atheism, have pretty much embraced the God-less moral theory held by atheists and agnostics. This third group may be described as "fellow-travelers" of atheists and agnostics. They may also be described as semi-atheists, for in their belief system they don't go all the way to atheism, but they come damn close. On a spectrum of belief—with orthodox Catholicism at one end and atheism at the other—liberal religion is notably closer to the atheist than to the Catholic end of the spectrum.

It is the worldview and moral values of this coalition—that is to say, a *secularist* worldview and morality—that have become culturally dominant in the United States in the last half-century, dethroning the Protestant worldview and morality that had been dominant throughout American history from the colonial era until the 1960s. A great cultural revolution took place in the United States in the 1960s and '70s, and you bishops did not really understand it. You noticed (who could not notice?) that there was a great expansion of sexual liberty; and you noticed that a right to abortion (a right to commit homicide against unborn babies) had become the law of the land; and you noticed that tolerance of homosexuality was on the rise (on the rise even among your diocesan priests and in your seminaries). But you didn't notice that these specific phenomena were part and parcel of a more general phenomenon, namely, a "war" against Catholicism and all forms of traditional or old-fashioned Christianity. Or if you noticed, you did little in the way of protecting the religion of your people.

Perhaps you will say that it would have been difficult, difficult almost to the point of impossibility, to do much that would have been effective. Maybe so; but Evangelical and Pentecostal Protestantism did not find it impossible. They recognized the danger, and they did much, and are still doing much, to resist it. While mainline Protestant denominations were shrinking during the last half-century, shrinking both as a percentage of the overall American population and in absolute numbers, Evangelical and Pentecostal churches (plus the Mormons) have been flourishing. They recognized the anti-Christianity enemy, and they fought back. They struggled to protect and build up the Christian faith of their people, and they struggled to push back the advancing cultural-political tide of anti-Christian secularism. Why couldn't the Catholic Church have done the same? Very probably it could have if it had been led by bishops up to the task.

When I say this, I don't mean to suggest that such a task of resistance would have been easy. Just the opposite—it would have been extraordinarily difficult. Catholic bishops in the 1960s and '70s and beyond faced tremendous opposition, both external and internal. On the external side, they were opposed by outright secularists (atheists and agnostics) plus the liberal Protestant and Jewish "fellow-travelers" of these secularists. And they were opposed as well by a generation of young people who, rebelling against the authority of their elders in church, state, university, and family, had discovered the joys of personal liberty generally and of sexual freedom in particular. Internally, you bishops were opposed by many priests and religious sisters who were inspired by a vague "spirit of Vatican II" and by equally vague notions of liberation theology that followed from that spirit; and you also faced internal opposition from laypersons of the "cafeteria Catholic" persuasion—that is, Catholics who were drifting more or less rapidly away from full-bodied Catholicism in the direction of an increasingly thin Generic Christianity. In the face of that kind of opposition, you bishops would have needed heroic qualities of leadership. But you were not heroic leaders; you were garden-variety leaders at best; and at worst many of your order were (please pardon me for saying this, but it's true) little better than cowardly.

Atheism and near-atheism is fertile cultural soil. And from this soil grows the tree of anti-Christianity; and this tree sprouts many branches, among them the branches of sexual freedom, abortion, and the approval, indeed the virtual glorification, of homosexuality. And there is another tree that grows right next to this first tree, the tree of watered-down Catholicism, aka Generic Christianity. All this has been happening right under the noses of you bishops, and you have done little about it. "You accuse us of not being heroes," you will say. "But to be a hero is to act above and beyond the call of duty. We did our duty. You can't blame us for not being heroic." Wrong. You can always blame the man at the top—indeed you *must* blame the man at the top—when his organization has a great failure. That's why baseball teams fire losing managers and football teams fire losing coaches. Normally heroism is a matter of going beyond the call duty; but sometimes heroism *is* the call of duty. The great American cultural revolution that began in the 1960s was one of those times. And you bishops failed.

What I'll be telling you

In this book (open letter), my dear bishops, I want to tell you two things that nobody should have to remind you of. In Part I, I'll remind you what kind of country you are living in. You are *not* living in the kind of America that once existed, the country of your parents, perhaps even (depending on your age) the country of your childhood. That is to say, you are not living in an America in which Protestantism is culturally dominant. It is true that a numerical majority of Americans are still Protestant (in one sense or another of that very elastic word), but the elites who now dominate American culture are no longer Protestant, no longer Christian. They are secularist; which is to say, they are atheists or agnostics who not only disbelieve in Christianity but are hostile to its doctrines and to much of its morality.

In Part II, I will offer a few suggestions about what you can do to get American Catholicism back on track. However, I will do this while acknowledging that nobody (certainly not myself) can lay out a blueprint for a future campaign to save American Catholicism. It is well to have a battle plan when one starts a campaign, but one has to remain flexible. Plans will have to change depending on circumstances, and the strategy that produces victory (if victory ever *is* produced) will probably be discovered someplace in the middle of the campaign.

[end of chapter]

PART ONE

THE SOCIETY
WE'RE LIVING IN

In this first part of the book I will offer a description and analysis of today's American society and culture insofar as these are relevant to the task you bishops face of defending the Church and its faith against the secularist worldview that is becoming increasingly influential in American life. In doing this I'll discuss the following: how Catholics were assimilated to American culture and as a result gave the Catholic Church in America a "Protestant" character (chapter 2); the nature of anti-Christian secularism (chapters 3 and 4); five stages of the history of the growth of secularism in the United States (chapter 5); the latest stage of secularism, outright atheism (chapter 6); and finally, the social basis of contemporary secularism, along with secularism's dominance in today's national Democratic Party—a party that has become an essentially anti-Christian party (chapter 7).

CHAPTER 2

Americanization & Protestantization

In recent decades a vast flood of immigrants to the United States, the great majority of them from Latin America, has led some Americans—Pat Buchanan being the most conspicuous among them[18]—to doubt that these tens of millions of newcomers can be successfully assimilated to American life and culture. This traditional American culture has been described by the late Harvard University professor Samuel Huntington, accurately in my opinion, as an "Anglo-Protestant" culture.[19] If the future turns out to be like the past, Latino and other newcomers will be assimilated; will be Americanized. But of course nobody can be sure this will happen, for nobody can clearly see the social-cultural future. But throughout its history, including its pre-independence colonial history, American society and culture have shown a tremendous capacity to absorb immigrant groups and transform them into full-fledged Americans. This history gives us strong reason to hope that our Anglo-Protestant culture can be preserved, regardless of the skin color or ethnic ancestry of the future American population.

---

[18] See Buchanan's book *Invasion*.
[19] See Huntington's book *Who Are We?*

It has usually taken a few generations for non-Americans to become fully Americanized. This Americanization process is perhaps most clearly illustrated by the example of language. Non-English-speaking immigrants have been transformed into English-only speakers, and this transformation has normally taken about three generations to be completed. Consider Italians as a typical non-English case. Migrants from Italy, mostly from the impoverished southern and Sicilian parts of that newly unified country, began arriving in the US in big numbers at the tail end of the 19th century, and they continued to arrive in big numbers until the outbreak of World War I. The first generation of immigrants—those who grew up in Italy and didn't come to the United States until they were adults—underwent only a small amount of Americanization during the remainder of their lives. They lived in Italian-speaking enclaves; as laborers, either skilled or unskilled, they worked at jobs that did not require much mastery of English; and as much as possible they retained their old world culture in their neighborhoods, their clubs, and their churches. A sign of this was the demand they usually made that their children marry within the Italian community. More than a few times this demand was unsuccessful, for their children—second-generation Americans—were already Americanizing; thinking of themselves as more American than Italian, many of them felt free to marry non-Italo-Americans. This second generation—the children who were born in, or at least grew up in, the United States—had one foot in each of two worlds, the old Italian world and the new American world. Accordingly, they were bilingual, speaking Italian at home, English at school and on the street with their playmates. Commonly they acted as translators for their parents. As they grew older and moved more and more out of the small world of their families and neighborhoods and into the larger outside world, their Italian language and culture came to play a smaller and smaller part in their lives; but these Italian features never totally disappeared; they always counted. Often, but certainly not always, the spouses of these second-generation Italo-Americans would also be Italo-Americans; or if not Italian, then at least Catholic. These second-generation Italians were sufficiently Americanized to marry outside their ethnic group but not so Americanized as to marry outside their religious group. The third generation—grandchildren of the original immigrants, children of those who had grown up in America—was thoroughly Americanized. English was their only language—except perhaps for a few prayers their grandmother taught them or a few swear words they picked up from their uncles. Marrying a non-Italian was no longer a rare thing. To be sure, not all traces of their Italian-ness vanished. But these traces were no more than that—traces. Overwhelmingly these people had become American in their language, beliefs, morals, manners, values, etc. They had been successfully Americanized.

As the Italian example illustrates, American culture has proven to be tremendously attractive, if not always to immigrants themselves, then to their children and grandchildren. Maybe the future will be different, but I can see no good reason for believing American culture will become less attractive in the future; if this is true, a process of relatively rapid assimilation will continue. Mexicans, Dominicans, Guatemalans, Brazilians, Africans, etc. will be Americanized within two or three generations.[20]

Our Anglo-Protestant Culture

As noted above, Samuel Huntington has called American culture Anglo-Protestant. No doubt this is a debatable label (all labels are debatable), but not *very* debatable. Nothing could be more obvious than the English element in our culture: our language, literature, law, system of government, political philosophy, etc.—all are derived from English originals. And the Protestant element is almost equally obvious: from the beginning the great majority of Americans have been Protestants of one kind or another. To be sure, the proportion of that majority has shrunk over the centuries. At the beginning of the republic, something not far from 99 percent of all Americans were Protestant; not necessarily church-going Protestants, but Protestant

---

[20] I concede however that the normal process of Americanization could be hindered if we have *too many* newcomers to process at the same time. But nobody really knows what "too many" is.

nonetheless. Today, by contrast, only about 2/3 of all Americans consider themselves Protestant; a smaller majority, but still a great majority.

However, we run into a sociological puzzle at this point. For if the United States has always been a Protestant country, and if newcomers to America— finding this new country and its culture, as I said, "tremendously attractive"— have been thoroughly Americanized within two or three generations, then how come the descendants of Catholic immigrants from Ireland, Italy, Germany, Poland, Portugal, Quebec, etc, along with the descendents of Jewish immigrants from Germany and the Russian Empire, have not all become Protestant? Very little of this has happened. They gave up their foreign languages in order to speak English, but very few Catholics or Jews have given up their foreign religion and joined Protestant churches.[21]

Protestantism, according to Huntington (and I agree with him), is an essential ingredient of American culture. But how can this be true if non-Protestant newcomers to the United States don't turn Protestant? If they have been truly Americanized, how can it be that they have not adopted the "essential" American religion? Appearances can be deceptive. It is my contention that Protestantization of American Catholics and Jews *has* taken place—though not because individual Catholics and Jews joined this or that Protestant church in large numbers. No, it has taken place because these non-Protestant religions have themselves taken on a decidedly Protestant coloring. Today American Catholicism is to a great degree a *Protestantized Catholicism*, and American Judaism is for the most part a *Protestantized Judaism*. There are holdouts of course: Catholics who are orthodox or traditional in their beliefs, morality, and devotional attitudes; and Orthodox and ultra-Orthodox Jews. But majorities in both non-Protestant groups have, without leaving their particular religion,

---

[21] An exception to this rule has recently occurred among recent immigrants from Latin America, many of whom have given up their hereditary Catholicism to join Evangelical or Pentecostal churches. Among the older immigrant groups from Europe, by contrast, joining a Protestant church was an exceedingly rare phenomenon. But the Latino tendency to convert to Evangelical or Pentecostal churches is not something that began in the United States. It is something that was going on, and is still going on, in their home countries in Latin America.

become Protestantized. Their "I am an American" tendency led them to adopt a Protestant religious mentality, but there was no need to leave their old religions in order to do this. Instead they transformed their old religions into quasi-Protestant faiths.

Let me explain. From the beginning of Protestantism in the 16th century, one of its distinctive features—a feature that just as clearly differentiated it from Catholicism as its rejection of the papacy, and was indeed the inevitable counterpart of its rejection of the papacy—has been its principle of *private judgment*. Having discarded the pope as the final authority in religion, Protestantism needed an alternative authority, and found it in the Bible. "The Bible, the whole Bible, and nothing but the Bible" soon became the ultimate religious authority for Protestants.[22] But this created a problem. It seems obvious—and this is what Catholic critics of Protestantism have always pointed out—that if twenty different people read the Bible, they may well come up with twenty different interpretations. How, then, can the Bible be an effective authority? Isn't it far more likely to be a principle of confusion and division? The Protestant answer to this objection was that if the twenty people read the Bible in the *right way*, they will *not* get twenty different interpretations; they will get one interpretation, and this will be the correct interpretation. And what is the "right way" to read the Bible? Well, it must be read carefully and with due attention given to the advice of experts (e.g., one's local pastor); above all it must be read prayerfully, keeping the mind open to the guidance of the Holy Spirit. It was the Holy Spirit who had been the true author of the Bible in the first place, and it is the Holy Spirit who can guide us to a true reading of the Bible today.

That was fine in theory, but in the real world things didn't work that way. Either because the theory was wrong, or because people didn't wait for the guidance of the Holy Spirit, or because the Holy Spirit's guidance wasn't equally available to all, what happened in practice was that private judgment led—just as Catholic critics had predicted—to many different readings of the

---

[22]   Or according to the famous saying of the 17th century English Protestant apologist Chillingworth: "The Bible is the religion of Protestants."

Bible and, consequently, to many different Protestant sects and denominations. In principle there is no reason it cannot lead to as many different versions of Christianity as there are individuals who read the Bible. Not every Protestant of course who has read the Bible for the past five centuries has come up with an individualized version of Christianity, but there have been countless individualized versions of it. In the century or two following the Reformation, attempts were made, by means of official state churches, to prevent the multiplication of sects; dissent was suppressed by silencing and punishing dissenters. For example, England's Queen Elizabeth (who reigned from 1558 to 1603) punished, sometimes even with death, Catholics (to her religious right) and Puritans (to her religious left) who for quite different reasons dissented from the Church of England. And in 17th century Massachusetts, government authorities expelled the dissenters Roger Williams and Ann Hutchinson, and on occasion punished Quakers with death. To a considerable degree these attempts at repression and restriction were successful, but not completely so; for the principle of private judgment was so deeply rooted in Protestantism that there was no eradicating its effects. Inevitably the principle produced, and is producing to this day, a multiplicity of sects and a vast number of individualized definitions of Christianity.

With time, the Protestant principle of private judgment spilled over into secular fields. People living in Protestant countries—in the United States, for example, the most Protestant of all Protestant countries: the northern colonies of America, as Edmund Burke put it in his Speech on Conciliation (March, 1775), were the home of "the dissidence of Dissent, the Protestantism of the Protestant religion"—decided that they had a right to think for themselves not just on religious questions but on all questions: moral questions, political questions, aesthetic questions, etc. And so today's Americans, continuing to think for themselves, reject authority on all subjects except mathematics and natural science. And even in science there is a certain amount of private judgment that takes place: for instance, some people feel free to reject the consensus of biologists regarding biological evolution, while others feel free to reject medical science as they pursue a variety of non-scientific (often quack) remedies for health problems.

Catholics, having become true Americans, are as likely as anyone else to "think for themselves." They think for themselves about politics, society, etc.—*and about morality and religion.* Like other Americans, they reject the idea that there is some external authority who can tell them how to think on these subjects; and from this it follows quite naturally and logically that they reject the teaching authority of bishops and popes.[23] Of course, they have a feeling of affection for the pope, just as Englishmen have a feeling of affection for the queen, and they are willing to give papal teachings a certain amount of respectful consideration; but they don't believe that the pope is an oracle of truth whose teachings must be accepted. In a pinch they are willing, out of respect, to call him "the Vicar of Christ," but they don't really believe this; for if he were truly Christ's vicar, his teachings—that is to say, the teachings of the Church—would have to be received as authoritative. For a true American, who is a believer in the right of private judgment, there are no teaching authorities outside the fields of mathematics and (for the most part) natural science. When the pope says, for instance, that it is sinful for a married couple to practice contraception, the typical American Catholic (who in this regard is far more American than Catholic) responds by saying: "Well, that's the opinion of the pope and the official Church. I love the Church, but it's a hopelessly out-of-date opinion, and I respectfully disagree."

Now a Church that is chiefly made up of members who "think for themselves" when it comes to questions of morality and religion may be the Catholic Church *in name*; it may even be the Catholic Church according to the intention of its members. But it is not the Catholic Church according to the Church's traditional and orthodox understanding of itself. For it is not a church in which bishops and popes are authoritative teachers. A church of this kind is, to repeat, a "Protestantized" Catholic Church.

The same is true of Judaism in America: it too got Protestantized—a Protestantized Judaism in which the individual Jew, while listening with

---

[23] I hasten to add that not *all* American Catholics are so attached to the Protestant principle of private judgment that they reject the authority of the pope. But it is a relatively rare American Catholic who accepts this authority in the spirit in which Rome intends it.

a certain amount of respect to the opinions of rabbis, thinks for himself. Traditional Judaism, that is, Rabbinic or Orthodox Judaism, is not a private judgment religion. It is, like orthodox Catholicism, a religion of authority: in its case the teaching authority of rabbis. In fact American Jews, apart from the small Orthodox minority in their ranks, are even more inclined than Catholics to think for themselves; more than a few Jews have carried thinking for themselves so far as to reject belief in God without at the same time rejecting their Jewish identity. Jews, in short, are even more "Protestant" than are Catholics. One of the reasons for this is that the first Jews to come to America in significant numbers were German Jews who arrived at the middle of the 19th century. The Judaism they brought with them from Germany, an intellectually advanced modern society, was Reform Judaism, that is, a very "liberal" kind of Judaism, a Judaism that had left Orthodox or Rabbinic Judaism far behind. When Orthodox Jews from the Russian Empire and other places in eastern and central Europe began to arrive in America in large numbers at the end of the 19th and beginning of the 20th centuries, they discovered that the Jewish "establishment" in America was religiously liberal. In the United States, Orthodox Judaism has always found it difficult to flourish or even to survive. Many Jews who grew up in Orthodox families have as teens or as adults drifted religiously to the "left," either to more liberal forms of Judaism (Reform or Conservative) or to outright non-religion.

It should be noted that the currently "Protestant" nature of the Catholic Church in the United States is not limited to the embrace of the principle of private judgment, even though this is the fundamental principle of Protestantized Catholicism. At the time of the Protestant Reformation of the 16th century, even though various forms of Protestantism emerged, forms that disagreed with one another—Lutheranism, Calvinism, Anglicanism, and a few others,—they all agreed in rejecting certain elements of Catholicism: (1) the authority of the pope, (2) mandatory priestly celibacy, (3) monasteries and convents, (4) the veneration of saints, (5) auricular confession, and (6) the use of Latin as the language of liturgy. In present-day American Catholicism all six of these old Protestant rejections have re-appeared.

1) As noted above, not many Catholics fully accept the authority of the pope;

2) while mandatory priestly celibacy has been retained (because Rome won't allow its abolition), most lay Catholics, according to public opinion polls, would like to allow married men to be priests;

3) monasteries and convents still exist, but the numbers of their inhabitants have declined sharply and are continuing to decline;

4) veneration of the saints is a rare thing nowadays;

5) the practice of confession/penance/reconciliation has largely vanished;

6) Latin has almost completely disappeared as a liturgical language.[24]

The drift toward irreligion

This, my dear bishops, is the kind of Catholic Church you have to deal with in America—a highly Protestantized church. "Well, that's not so bad," you might say. "We can live with that, provided that American Catholics, no matter how Protestant their attitude toward Christianity may be, continue to identify with the Catholic Church. Maybe someday—fifty years from now, a hundred years, two hundred years, who knows?—these Protestantized Catholics will once again become real Catholics."

But it *is* bad, and this for three reasons.

For one thing, Protestantism and Catholicism, no matter how much they have in common, *really are* different from one another, historically, doctrinally, and even morally. If the Catholic Church in America drifts more and more in a Protestant direction, this will be tantamount to drifting further and further from Catholicism. It will become a Catholic Church in name only, a Catholic Church without the Catholicism. The Catholic religion, as a unique and distinctive thing, will have disappeared.

---

[24] Unlike the other rejections, which were produced mainly by lay Catholics, the abolition of Latin was produced by Church authorities. Standing alone, it would have been unobjectionable. But combined with the other rejections, it contributed to move Catholicism in a Protestant direction.

For another, the kind of Protestantism that American Catholicism comes more and more to look like is not *Evangelical* Protestantism, which, no matter how objectionable from a strictly Catholic point of view, adheres to the articles of the Nicene Creed.[25] No, American Catholicism is coming to resemble "mainline" American Protestantism, and the mainline denominations, under the influence of liberal or modernistic Christianity, have been drifting away from traditional/orthodox Christianity for much more than 100 years now; with the velocity of that drift having accelerated in the last 50 years. The Christian content of mainline Protestantism has been growing thinner and thinner. Hence to the degree that Catholicism apes mainline Protestantism, Catholicism's Christian content too becomes thinner and thinner.

Finally, liberal Protestantism (the kind of Protestantism present-day American Catholics are aping), when its 200-year history is examined, is usually a halfway house—a semi-comfortable wayside inn—on the road from traditional Christianity to outright secularism and atheism. It is a logically incoherent attempt to find a middle ground between Christianity and the anti-Christian secularism that happens to be fashionable at the moment.[26] Thus early 19th century Unitarianism was a middle ground between Christianity and Deism. The modernistic Protestantism of the late 19th and early 20th centuries was a middle ground between Christianity and agnosticism. And the liberal Christianity of the last 30 or 40 years has been a middle ground between Christianity and sexual liberationism. As secularism moves further and further to the "left," liberal religion moves with it. To travel in a single leap from Catholicism to atheism is not, psychologically speaking, an easy thing to do. But to go from liberal religion to atheism is a relatively easy transition; something of a downhill slide. A Catholicism that is liberal, on the model of liberal Protestantism, will find that it is an excellent preparatory school for

---

[25] Unlike Catholicism, Evangelical Protestantism does not accept the Nicene Creed as authoritative; only the Bible is accepted as authoritative. But this is a formal, not a substantive, difference between Catholicism and Evangelical Protestantism; for Evangelicals find all the teachings of the Creed in the Bible.

[26] I'll have more to say about this in chapter five, below.

atheism; and if liberal Catholics themselves don't slide into atheism, many of their children and grandchildren will.

In short, my dear bishops, you are losing your church. It is slipping away from you. What do you propose to do about this?

[end of chapter]

CHAPTER 3

Today's Enemy

For centuries the great enemy of Catholicism was Protestantism. In the time following the commencement of the Protestant Reformation (conventionally dated from the moment Martin Luther posted his 95 theses on the church door at Wittenberg, late October 1517), Catholicism not only lost its religious monopoly in Western Europe, it came perilously close to destruction. Protestantism won half of Germany, much of France, most of Switzerland, plus all of Scandinavia, England, Scotland, and the United Provinces (Holland). A generation or so after the onset of the Reformation, the Catholic Church rallied, a rally that has been labeled the Counter-Reformation—which may be briefly if somewhat inadequately summed up as: *Trent plus the Jesuits*. This rally halted the Protestant advance, and the struggle between the two religions, though still intense, tended toward stalemate.

Beginning with the French Revolution (1789), or rather, beginning with the intellectual buildup to the Revolution (Voltaire, Diderot, Rousseau, et al., all of whom flourished in the middle years of the 18th century), Catholicism faced a second great enemy, anti-Christian secularism.[27] Throughout the 19th

---

[27] I'll describe the nature of secularism at greater length in chapters 4, 5, and 6. For the time being, suffice it to say that secularism in the Western world has always involved, not just disbelief in the distinctive teachings of Christianity, but also great hostility to Christianity, viewing it as a pernicious religion.

and early 20th centuries, secularism replaced Protestantism as the Catholic Church's principal enemy in Europe. Protestantism had grown old and a bit tired by that time: the fight between the two religions had long since reached stalemate. But the new enemy, secularism, was full of energy, and it especially flourished in historically Catholic countries, e.g., Spain, Italy, and above all France. In the 20th century still newer enemies—enemies that were both secularist and totalitarian—appeared: moderately anti-Catholic Fascism in Italy, strongly anti-Christian Nazism in Germany, and the most furiously anti-Christian enemy of all, Communism in Russia and almost everywhere else in Europe. By this time the old enemy, Protestantism, seemed a pretty tame thing in comparison with these newer enemies.

But not in the United States. Here during the 19th and much of the 20th centuries, there was a certain amount of secularism, but not much; hardly anything at all in comparison with the potent secularism found in Europe. As for totalitarianism, there was, it is true, an American Communist Party that was more than a merely negligible factor in our national life during the 1930s and '40s and early '50s; still, it was a minor thing, and very few Catholics were tempted to join the party. Here in the United States Protestantism remained the number one enemy of Catholicism. That is to say: if there was a danger that Catholics might defect from the Catholic Church to something else, in America this "something else" would be Protestantism; it would not be liberal secularism or totalitarian secularism. Let the Church in Europe fight Communism and Nazism and anticlericalism; here in America the Church would remain on guard against its old enemy, Protestantism.

Sexual and moral liberalism

All this changed beginning in the 1960s. Suddenly, during the cultural revolution of the '60s and '70s ("drugs, sex, rock 'n' roll"—the modern naughty trinity, the equivalent of the ancient naughty trinity of "wine, women, and song"), a new kind of secularism emerged. Let's call it "moral secularism," or perhaps better, "sexual secularism." During the so-called sexual revolution of the '60s and '70s, conduct that had been taboo in Christian societies from time out of mind—premarital sex, casual sex, unmarried cohabitation, out-of-wedlock motherhood, abortion, homosexuality, pornography, etc.— suddenly, almost overnight it seemed, became widely acceptable, especially among those who were young and sexually adventurous. Hitherto the secularists of the American world had been brainy and highly educated people who wrote and read books "proving" the falsity of Christianity and all other supernatural religions, "proving" that Christianity is a religion based on nothing more than superstition, wishful thinking, and fraud. But the new secularists—the sexual revolutionaries—had no need to write or to read books. All they had to do was to go bed with somebody they weren't married to, frankly admitting this, or boasting about it, to friends and acquaintances, or even better, to Mom and Dad; all the while having a good conscience about fornication. They were repudiating the Christian sexual ethic. More significantly, since this ethic was an essential and important part of Christianity, in repudiating the sexual ethic of Christianity they were repudiating Christianity itself, declaring it in effect to be a false morality and false religion, an exploded mythology. The implied syllogism, which I spoke of earlier in the book, went like this:

- If Christianity is true, then fornication, cohabitation, abortion, etc. are wrong.
- But they are *not* wrong.
- Therefore Christianity is not true.

This is a valid argument in the form *modus tollens* (as it is called in logic textbooks).

Let me underline the point that these sexual revolutionaries were doing more, very much more, than merely committing what Catholics and other traditional Christians counted as sexual sins. More important, they were *denying* that these "sins" are sinful. The commission of sexual sin was nothing new, nor was it especially harmful to the Church. Christians had been committing sexual sins from the beginning of Christianity; and since the Catholic Church offers remedies for sins, then sexual sins, it may be said, help keep the Church in business—much as illness keeps doctors and hospitals in business, and as crime keeps police officers and prisons in business. Do away with illness, and you'll have no more need for doctors or hospitals; do away with crime, and you'll have no more need for police and prisons. Likewise, do away with sin, and you'll have no more need for the Catholic Church. The sexual revolutionaries of the '60s and '70s got rid of the sin of unmarried sex, not by abstaining from it, but by declaring it to be un-sinful. Earlier fornicators had said to themselves, "This is wrong, I admit, but it's a pleasant thing to do; so I'll do it anyway." The new and up-to-date fornicator said: "This is a pleasant thing to do. And what's more, it isn't wrong. Just the opposite, it's natural and right." The revolutionaries were not so much *breaking* the rules of Christian morality as they were *repudiating* these rules, rejecting them as nonsensical and inhumane. They were proclaiming a new morality that was thoroughly antithetical to Catholic morality. From the point of view of Catholicism and any other old-fashioned version of Christianity (e.g., Evangelical Protestantism), they were, to use a technically correct but rather outdated term, moral *heretics*.

This new secularism didn't stop at being a sexual revolution. It justified its sexual conduct by adopting a principle of morality that justified this sexual conduct. But this was a universal principle intended to apply to *all* conduct, not just sexual conduct. According to this universal principle, conduct is morally permissible provided it doesn't harm non-consenting others—and by "harm" was usually understood pain and suffering, including those injuries (e.g., theft) that bring about pain and suffering. Let's call this rule, that we are morally free to do anything that doesn't harm another, the Personal Liberty Principle (PLP). This was one side of a coin, the other side of which was the Tolerance Principle (TP), according to which we have a duty to tolerate all forms of conduct provided that this conduct does no harm to non-consenting others. We may call the combination of these two principles—the PLP plus the TP—*moral liberalism*.[28]

---

[28] For those revolutionaries who liked to read theoretical books, a classic statement of moral liberalism, or at least something very like it, could be found in John Stuart Mill's *On Liberty,* first published in 1859.

But once you become a moral liberal and adopt the PLP and TP, you find that you can justify much more than fornication. You can justify homosexual behavior. You can justify abortion too (provided of course that you take care, thanks to a rather impressive act of self-deception, not to count the entity killed in an abortion as a human person). You can justify suicide. And if you can justify suicide, then you can justify assisted suicide, that is, voluntary euthanasia; and in some cases—e.g., cases in which a terminally ill person has lost the capacity for rational decision-making—you can justify *involuntary* euthanasia. And of course you can justify adultery, provided you make sure that the "injured" spouse either gives permission (express or implied) or doesn't guess that the adultery is actually taking place. Further, if you can break the promises contained in wedding vows, you can break other promises as well, provided nobody is hurt. Likewise you can tell lies, provided your lies cause no pain or suffering to anybody. For in all these cases no harm—so at least it is argued—is done to innocent third parties.

In opposition to moral liberalism, it can of course be argued that the many "sins" mentioned above are *not* harmless to non-consenting parties. It is not very difficult to make out a plausible case that fornication, cohabitation, secret adultery, homosexuality, suicide, lying, etc. cause great social harm. The only way moral liberals can use the PLP and TP to justify these forms of conduct is by taking a very truncated view of the consequences of such conduct. If the sky does not immediately fall,[29] then the conduct is judged to be harmless. Moral liberals typically exhibit scant curiosity about the indirect and long-term harmful consequences of conduct they approve of; only immediate and obvious consequences count.

---

[29] This is one of the most common justifications offered for same-sex marriage. We are often asked in so many words to note that "the sky hasn't fallen" in Massachusetts (and a few other states) despite SSM having been legal there for a number of years. But of course nobody on the anti-SSM side argues that the socially harmful consequences of SSM will become immediately obvious. "The sky hasn't fallen" argument commits the textbook fallacy of *ignoratio elenchi*—the fallacy of "refuting" an argument that nobody has offered.

What is especially odd about this truncated view is that many moral liberals are the same persons who are masterful at tracing long-term and indirect consequences when it comes, say, to protecting the physical environment. They can trace the connection between my automobile's gasoline consumption and the melting of polar ice caps—yet somehow they can't see, for instance, that an ethic of sexual permissiveness has led to millions of fatherless children who grow up in neighborhoods that are impoverished and drug-and-crime-infested; nor can they see that it has led to a vast epidemic of sexually transmitted diseases. Or if they see these results, then either they don't care, or they propose unrealistic or even harmful remedial action. For instance, they propose that all teenage kids be provided with free-of-charge condoms and morning-after pills; or they propose that welfare payments and taxpayer-provided day-care for working mothers make up for absent fathers. In his Inaugural Address in 2013, President Obama, whose viewpoint often represents the mindset of the moral liberals who helped to put him in office (think of his support for abortion rights and homosexuality and same-sex marriage), called for universal pre-K. This is a program that moral liberals believe will, among other things, nullify the potentially harmful effects of out-of-wedlock births and fatherless homes. If at the moment absentee fatherhood is causing harm to children, this is not, liberals believe (or pretend to believe), the result of the sexual permissiveness encouraged by moral liberalism; it is the result of the backwardness of Christian and other moral conservatives, who block pre-K and other welfare programs to assist unmarried mothers and their children.

You'd think that moral liberals would at least recognize that *abortion* does harm to another person. After all, it kills an unborn human being, doesn't it? There are numerous strategies of self-deception that moral liberals have available to them when defending their prochoice (pro-abortion) position—all of these strategies reeking of intellectual dishonesty. (1) Sometimes prochoice persons commit an astonishing act of self-deception: they simply deny, against all the biological evidence, that the aborted entity is a human being. (2) Another strategy is simply to *ignore* the question of whether or not the aborted entity is human. One simply refuses to think about it. (3) Yet another strategy focuses on the idea that the entity experiences no pain when destroyed by abortion—it feels no pain because it lacks the nervous system needed to experience either pain or pleasure.[30] And since the PLP says that an act is morally permissible so long as it doesn't cause harm to another—that is, pain or suffering—then it follows that the violent destruction of an unborn baby is morally permissible. It is very doubtful, however, that anybody truly believes that the only moral question that matters is the question of pain. Even the most ardent prochoice person must realize that it is wrong to take the life of an innocent human being even when that life can be taken without causing pain. Murder is still murder even if you take the trouble to sedate the victim before blowing his brains out. (4) Yet another strategy is to treat the abortion as a kind of euthanasia, a mercy killing. The life of the child, if the child were permitted to be born, would be so unpleasant that the child would better off dead. Of course, we cannot ask the unborn child if he or she would prefer to be killed. And so we (the mother, the abortionist, et al.), acting as trustees for the child's welfare, substitute our judgment for the child's. But it is absurd to believe that the unborn children killed in abortion would, if they could, give their consent to the abortion. Can anybody honestly believe that the child would say: "Oh, yes, please kill me—lest I be born to an unwed teenager, or be born in poverty, or be born with a physical handicap, or be born to a career woman whose career would be interrupted by my arrival in the world, etc., etc."? (5) Or one shifts attention from the entity killed in an abortion to the plight of the unhappy woman choosing to abort. One feels great compassion for the poor woman (and indeed she is often in a situation deserving of great compassion), and tells oneself that her situation is so sad that it makes it unnecessary to worry about the situation of the entity being killed. (6) Moral liberals think of themselves as progressives, and they believe in something very like a theory of inevitable progress: the new is always better than the old. Many liberals, if you corner them, will admit that there are moments of retrogression, that not everything new is better than everything old; they will acknowledge, when reminded of Hitler and his followers, that the coming of Nazism to Germany was a moment

---

[30]   That the victim experiences no pain is no doubt true in the case of the great majority of abortions, though it is very doubtful in the case of late-term abortions.

of retrogression. But they cannot help but feeling that this is a great exception to the rule, and that the general rule is that the world gets better and better all the time. Belief in the moral rightness and goodness of abortion is a new belief, therefore a true belief. It is a belief that is on "the right side of history" (one of the favorite expressions of liberals when determining what's morally right and what's morally wrong). Again, how can an intellectually honest person judge the moral goodness or badness of conduct on the basis of what's up-to-date?

How can anybody, even an ardent prochoice person, not know that the question of the ontological status of the entity being killed in abortion—is this a human being, or is it something else?—matters, and matters above all other questions? Only a profound act of intellectual dishonesty can lead someone to blink the question of the humanity/non-humanity of the fetus. But this act of intellectual dishonesty is committed a billion times a day by America's moral liberals. How odd that activist defenders of abortion, who on average have higher levels of formal education than persons active in the prolife movement, should be guilty of such an intellectual crime.

What's really going on here is *not* that the new secularists have discovered a moral theory (namely, moral liberalism) that they feel bound to adopt because of its obvious truth. No, they feel compelled to adopt it because it allows them to repudiate Christianity and traditional Christian morality, especially Christian sexual morality; it gives them a convenient stick with which to beat traditional Christian morality. If it had been a traditional teaching of Christianity that SUVs are bad because they damage the environment, moral liberals would suddenly not be able to notice that SUVs damage the environment.

Far more dangerous than Protestantism

This cultural revolution of the 1960s was by far the most dangerous attack made on Catholicism in the history of the United States—yet somehow you bishops didn't understand this. Or if you understood it, you didn't act effectively to defend against it. The older attack on Catholicism, i.e., the attack made by 19th century Protestantism, was moderate in comparison. Protestants denounced certain aspects of Catholicism—the papacy, the veneration of saints, auricular confession, the ideal of celibacy and lifelong virginity, etc. But they didn't denounce Catholicism root and branch, because most of the roots and branches of Catholicism were also roots and branches of Protestantism. They couldn't say Catholicism was *totally* wrong without saying that their own religion was *almost totally* wrong. But this new attack, the one being made by secularist moral liberals of the 1960s and '70s, was a root-and-branch attack. It was not an attack on Catholicism in particular; it was a generalized attack on all forms of Christianity, Catholic, Protestant, and Orthodox, not to mention certain newer forms like Mormonism. But you Catholic bishops, who in the old days had done an excellent job of defending Catholicism against the moderate attacks made by Protestantism, have done a remarkably poor job of defending Catholicism against the far more radical attacks made by late 20th century secularism.

I should note (a point to be expanded upon later) that the secularist attack on Christianity was to a great degree limited to what may be called conservative Christianity, e.g., Catholicism and old-school Protestantism (Evangelicalism). Secularism did not attack liberal Christianity, or at least the attack on liberal Christianity was mild, so mild that one hardly noticed it. Why? Because liberal Christianity,[31] from the time of its first appearing in the world a little more than 200 years ago, has always been an attempt to blend Christianity with whatever happened to be the fashionable secularism (or anti-Christianity) of the day. Such an attempt is of course incoherent: it is like attempting to blend fire and water. But it has happened again and again as liberal Christians have said to themselves: "I hate to give up Christianity, it is such a lovely thing; but our critics make some very good points; so let's see if I can modernize my

---

[31] By "liberal Christianity" I mean, following the lead of John Henry Newman, a form of Christianity that has in effect repudiated the dogmatic principle in religion. Liberal Christianity holds that the individual Christian is free to believe or disbelieve whatever he likes; he is free, for all practical purposes, to invent his own version of Christianity. This is simply the old Protestant principle of *private judgment* run wild. Conservative Protestants also adhere in theory to the principle of private judgment, but in practice try to limit its effects.

religion and make it less vulnerable to modern criticism." And so the earliest American liberal Christians, the Boston Unitarians of the first decades of the 19th century, attempted to blend Christianity with Deism. And when in the late 19th century Christianity came under attack from agnostics, liberal Christians, in a bow to the agnostic theory of knowledge, agreed that God is not an object of knowledge so much as an object of feeling. And so, in the last third of the 20th century, when Christianity came under attack from a kind of secularism that denounced in a general way the moral principles of Christianity and in a particular way its sexual morality, liberal Christians once again said what they always say ("Our critics make a good point, etc."), and they proceeded to find justifications for fornication, cohabitation, homosexuality, same-sex marriage, abortion, and so on. Why would secularists bother to find fault with this kind of "Christianity"? Liberal Christians are to outright anti-Christian secularists what, 70 or 80 years ago, "pink" fellow-travelers were to "red" Communists. Or, to change the analogy, liberal Christians are to outright secularists what "enablers" are to alcoholics or drug addicts.

The perfect storm (1): Vatican II

How could you bishops have failed to recognize the danger posed by secularism and its philosophy of moral liberalism? I suppose if secularists had been like Russian Communists, arresting priests and shooting them, you would have recognized the enemy and put up a valiant defense. But your far more subtle enemy, the moral liberal (who, no matter how much he deplores priests, wouldn't dream of shooting them), somehow slipped under your pastoral radar. How?

I suppose the simplest answer to this is that the bishops of the immediate post-Vatican II era were so focused on internal difficulties that they had no eyes for external threats. The Second Vatican Council ended in late 1965, and even before ending it had, in combination with other factors, begun to cause great commotions in the Church. Within a few years many priests left the priesthood, and many nuns fled the convent; and new recruits to replace the nuns and priests who had left, as well as the ones who were growing old and dying, were hard to find. To this day they remain hard to find. Church attendance went way down. Catholic schools were closing left and right. The practice of confession (penance, reconciliation) virtually disappeared. Almost all Catholics, aided and abetted by many priests and theologians, freely dissented from Church teaching on birth control, a teaching that seemed to most of them quite nonsensical. Given all this in-house turmoil and distress, how could you bishops take note of the growing secularist threat? When a man's house is on fire, he may not notice that somebody is out in the driveway stealing his car.

It is customary for conservative/orthodox American Catholics who lament the decline of the Church that began in the '60s to place the blame for this decline on Vatican II. Not all of them go so far as to wish that the Council had never taken place, though many do have that wish; but they universally deplore the "progressive" interpretation (or misinterpretation, they would argue) of the Council. Progressives had the habit—for that matter, they still have it—of speaking of "the spirit of the Council." The Council reformed many things; so its "spirit" was a spirit of reform. And this spirit implied (so progressives argue) a continuing program of reform that would have to go well beyond the literal and limited reforms made by the Council itself. The spirit of reform demands (according to this progressive interpretation of the Council) that priestly celibacy be merely optional; that women be ordained to the priesthood; that homosexuality be no bar to priestly ordination; that the ecclesiastical powers of the laity be greatly strengthened; that bishops be locally elected; that the pope renounce his dictatorial powers; that theological free speech be tolerated in the Church; that other religions, both Christian and non-Christian, be treated as the equals of Catholicism; that the idea of the infallibility of the Church and the pope be dropped; that marital contraception be allowed; that the taboos against premarital sex and homosexuality be softened; that abortion be dropped as an important political issue; that same-sex marriage be allowed by civil law if not by Church law; and so on. So runs the progressive agenda. All this dubious Catholicism and outright anti-Catholicism, say the conservatives, is the unhappy result of Vatican II.

I disagree. I grant that Vatican II was part of the problem—but only a part; not the whole thing. The great decline of Catholicism in America took place in the immediate aftermath of the Council, true, but to conclude from that chronological fact that it happened *because* of the Council is to commit the fallacy that logic textbooks call *post hoc, ergo propter hoc*—"after this, therefore because of this." I have argued elsewhere[32] that the decline was the result of a "perfect storm" involving three simultaneously converging factors, only one of which was Vatican II.

The perfect storm (2): end of the Catholic ghetto

A second factor in the decline of American Catholicism was the demise of the so-called "Catholic ghetto." To be sure, it wasn't a true ghetto, like the Jewish ghettos of earlier centuries, that is, an enclave effectively cut off from most of the social and cultural life of the larger society. It was at most a quasi-ghetto—a cultural enclave whose metaphorical walls were low and easy to jump over if that's what you wanted to do. In the 19th century, to protect Catholic immigrants and their children from what was perceived as the pernicious influence of Protestantism, which was of course the religion of the great majority of the American people and of the nation's social, cultural, economic, and political elites, those who led the Catholic Church in the United States—that is, bishops, priests, nuns—created an alternative Catholic "world" within the larger American world: something of an *imperium in imperio*. The possibility of creating this semi-separate Catholic world was facilitated by the fact that the American Catholic Church of the 19th century was dominated by Irish bishops, priests, and nuns; and in Ireland the leadership of the Catholic Church had more than a century's experience of keeping Catholics from being converted to the religion of their Protestant rulers and landlords. The construction of a Catholic ghetto in the United States was also made easier by

---

[32] See my book, *The Decline and Fall of the Catholic Church in America*: Sophia Institute Press, 2003.

the fact that American Protestants had, to say the least, a less than welcoming attitude toward Catholics: it was easier for Catholic shepherds to keep their flock inside the smaller Catholic world when Protestants did not invite them into the larger American world. This anti-Catholic prejudice of Protestants was the continuation of an old tradition of Anglo-American anti-Catholicism, a tradition that went back to the age of Queen Elizabeth I and her father Henry VIII.

The Catholic "ghetto" was successful in the sense that it kept almost all Catholics within the fold; hardly anybody turned Protestant. But it also succeeded in another way, in an American way rather than a Catholic way. That is, it helped transform foreigners into true Americans in everything but church membership, getting them ready for the day when they would be integrated into the mainstream of American social and cultural life. The Catholic Church in the United States was a great Americanization machine. The day for fully entering the mainstream finally arrived in the two decades immediately following World War II. A Catholic was elected president of the United States, a clear signal that Protestants were ready to recognize Catholics as full-fledged Americans. This was the signal Catholics had been waiting for. They threw down the walls of their quasi-ghetto and entered the mainstream of American life.

When it came to religion, the mainstream was still Protestant: this was *not* of course Fundamentalist or Evangelical Protestantism, but mainline Protestantism. (This mainline Protestant dominance of American life was on the verge of changing, as we'll see in a moment; but in the early '60s American culture was still dominated by mainline Protestantism.) So when Catholics fully entered American cultural life, they adopted something very like a modernized Protestant religious mentality. They didn't abandon the Catholic Church, to be sure, but they brought into the Church this liberal Protestant mentality and the Generic Christianity that went with it, and they began to wish that the Catholic Church could be transformed in such a way as to suit this mentality. Catholics of the 1960s, in sum, were on their way to becoming Generic Christians, and they wanted the Church to change with them. You bishops offered little resistance to this wish.

The perfect storm (3): the cultural/sexual revolution

A third factor was the great cultural revolution of the '60s and '70s, already referred to above. At its most obvious level it was a sexual revolution, but it was more than a sexual revolution; it was the triumph of a new kind of secularism, the triumph of moral liberalism. It started with the young, but its ideas and values soon spread well beyond the young; it "percolated" upward, so to speak. Although older people, at least the great majority of them, were not ready to become active participants in the sexual revolution, all the same they began losing confidence in many of their old moral convictions; what had previously seemed to them matters of principle now often seemed nothing more than matters of old-fashioned prejudice and timidity. Moral liberalism—the theory that you are morally free to do whatever you want as long as you don't harm non-consenting others—was on its way to replacing traditional Christian morality as America's dominant ethical theory. And so it was, at the very moment when Catholics were fully entering the American cultural mainstream, that the mainstream itself was in process of changing from a predominantly Protestant thing to a predominantly secularist thing.

Incidentally, it was Protestantism itself—liberal Protestantism, that is—that paved the way for this transformation. For liberal Protestantism prided itself on its tolerance; this was its great title to moral superiority. It was ready to tolerate everything except intolerance. This explains why it was *not* tolerant of Fundamentalism/Evangelicalism, which it regarded as religiously intolerant; nor until the 1960s had it been tolerant of Catholicism, which exhibited its intolerance by claiming to be "the one true Church." Now that the Catholics of the 1960s had become semi-Protestant and were soft-peddling their "one true Church" claim, liberal Protestantism found to its delight that it could at long last tolerate Catholics and Catholicism. Then along came the new secularists, i.e., sexual revolutionaries and moral liberals, and they pushed tolerance to new extremes. They created new frontiers of tolerance, granting moral legitimacy to behavior which until now everybody, or at least nearly everybody, had considered beyond the pale. How could liberal Protestants, those virtuosi of tolerance, hold out against this newer and braver form of tolerance? Some of these hitherto liberal Protestants went over to secularism totally, abandoning the thin and watery Christianity they had held until now. Others—employing the classic *via media* strategy that has always been employed by liberal Protestantism—invented a compromise between their watery Christianity and the values of moral liberalism: they gave their blessing, framed in the language of Christian piety and charity, to fornication, abortion, and homosexuality, although they did so with less enthusiasm than that typical of outright secularists. Others again, suspended (like Buridan's famous ass) between their commitment to tolerance on the one hand and their disgust at the new morality on the other, did nothing; they didn't endorse the new morality, but they didn't oppose it either. They just stood on the sidelines, dumbfounded and paralyzed

At all events, liberal Protestantism did almost nothing to resist the new morality and often collaborated with it. And since Catholicism, once the walls of its ghetto had been thrown down, drifted in the direction of becoming a copy of liberal Protestantism, many Catholics (perhaps most) likewise did nothing to resist the new morality; and they too, now that they were liberal quasi-Protestants, often collaborated with the new morality.

Soon secularism, moral liberalism, and an attitude of tremendous sexual tolerance became dominant in the more influential circles of American cultural life, from where it spread rather quickly to all spheres of American society. This dominance has continued to the present day. Today it is stronger than ever, now that the young cultural revolutionaries of the '60s are the mature men and women who control many of the great institutions of American life. In particular they dominate what may be called the three "command posts" of American culture: the national press (also known as the mainstream media), the elite colleges and universities (including law schools), and the entertainment industry. In their mature years these old cultural revolutionaries may be much less devoted to the practice of sexual freedom than they were in their salad days, but they remain devoted in principle to sexual freedom and, more importantly, to the abstract and very un-Christian principle that they have used to justify sexual freedom, namely the Personal Liberty Principle.

———

In sum, it wasn't Vatican II alone that caused the decline of the Catholic religion in the United States. Rather it was a convergence of three factors, a "perfect storm" made up of (1) Vatican II, (2) the end of the Catholic ghetto, and (3) the cultural revolution of the '60s and '70s. All by itself, Vatican II would have been mildly disruptive, but nothing more. When, by a piece of extraordinary historical bad luck, it interacted with the other two factors, it helped produce an ecclesiastical catastrophe.

[end of chapter]

CHAPTER 4

The Nature of Secularism

Before talking at greater length about Catholicism's secularist enemy, which I plan to do in this chapter, I must pause for a moment to deal with a likely objection to what I'll have to say. It is in my opinion a silly objection, a very silly objection indeed—but it's the kind of objection that Christians of a sentimental type, of whom there are many in the world, are prone to make. It goes like this: "Christianity is a religion of love and peace. It is wrong therefore for us Christians to think in terms of enemies and struggles against enemies. We shouldn't be dividing mankind into friends and foes. We should follow Jesus in recognizing all humans as our brothers and sisters. We should promote unity, not division."

Let's leave aside the fact that Christ is reported to have said that he came to bring not peace but a sword; and leave aside the further fact that he seems to have treated Pharisees and Sadducees as enemies of his good news; and leave aside the still further fact that throughout the entire history of Catholicism, including the history of apostolic times, there has never been a period in which the Church did not struggle against an "ideological" enemy, whether that enemy was paganism or heresy or Judaism or Islam or Protestantism or anticlericism or Communism. I will mention only three things. (1) The fact that you would like to have no enemies doesn't mean that you won't have enemies. It takes two to tango, including the lovely tango of peace and harmony and universal brotherhood. If the secularist decides to be an enemy of Christianity, then you as a Christian have an enemy whether you want one or not. (2) If you don't fight back against the cultural advance of secularism, you will be defeated; that is, Christianity will be defeated, losing more and more of its people, especially its young people, to the secularist crusade. Your unwillingness to fight is tantamount to surrender; worse still, it is tantamount to helping the enemy. (3) The "fight" I'm talking about is a metaphorical fight. I am not calling for the use of physical violence. Nor are our secularist enemies, who are very civilized in an upper-middle class kind of way, the kind of persons definitely not prepared to resort to physical violence. They are prepared, however, to resort to legal and governmental coercion, compelling Catholic and Evangelical and Mormon taxpayers to pay for pro-homosexual propaganda in public schools, for abortion, and for the contraceptives needed to facilitate widespread fornication, especially among teenagers. The fight I am talking about is, to repeat, a strictly metaphorical fight, to be carried on, not with bombs or prisons or thumbscrews, but with prayer and persuasion and self-defense in courtrooms and other forums.

A definition of secularism

In the preceding chapter I gave a partial description of contemporary American secularism. In this I want to elaborate upon that description by giving it in a more thorough, systematic, and definitive way. The typical American secularist today has five leading characteristics: in addition to being a moral liberal, he or she is an atheist, is hostile to Christianity, holds a skeptical theory of knowledge, and holds a naturalistic metaphysics. Let me talk about each of these points. It should be needless to add, but I'll add it anyway, that when I say these are the characteristics of the "typical" secularist, I don't mean to say that each and every secularist bears all five of these marks. I just mean to say that if you wish to paint a picture of the average secularist you'll have to take note of these five marks. Let me also add that I am here talking about outright secularists, not about the semi-secularists who are found among liberal religious believers. I'll talk about them later.

1. Atheism. Secularists are atheists or agnostics. Agnosticism, which strictly speaking holds that we humans are unable to answer the question of whether God exists or not, theoretically covers a broad spectrum of attitudes, a spectrum that touches on atheism at one end and theism at the other. You can be a religious agnostic, like the French Catholic thinker Blaise Pascal (1623-62), holding that there is no rational or philosophical answer to the question of God's existence, while at the same time choosing to *believe* in God. Or like the great 20ᵗʰ century Swiss Protestant theologian, Karl Barth, who held that it is impossible for unaided human reason to attain knowledge of God, and that all human knowledge of God comes from Revelation alone: we humans don't discover God, according to Barth—instead God reveals himself to us. Nowadays agnostics of this religious kind are rarely called agnostics; more often they are called *fideists*, a word derived from the Latin word "fides" ("faith"). Near the other end of the agnostic section of the theism/atheism spectrum, you can be a virtually atheistic agnostic, holding that, in the absence of a rational/ philosophical proof of God's existence, we should presume that God does not exist, and live and think accordingly. Our American agnostic secularists today are for the most part agnostics of this second kind, the virtual-atheist variety. As an abstract proposition they will concede that God *may* exist; after all, who can say for sure that he (or she or it) doesn't? Yet, they contend, there is no evidence, at least nothing like sufficient evidence, for God's existence. They further hold that intellectually careful and honest persons will proportion their assent to the evidence available.[33] Thus, in the absence of evidence that X is the case, a person of intellectual integrity will refuse to believe X. And so,

---

[33] The classic philosophical account of this attitude of proportioning assent to evidence is given in John Locke's *Essay concerning Human Understanding*, at the beginning of chapter 19 of book IV. The best-known Catholic rebuttal of Locke's view is given in Cardinal Newman's *Grammar of Assent*. William James, while not referring to Locke by name, offered another rebuttal in his famous essay, "The Will to Believe." (Locke nonetheless believed in God, for he thought the evidence for God's existence was sufficient to justify belief.)

while there may be a one-in-a-thousand or one-in-a-million chance that God exists, we must presume, in the absence of evidence for his existence, that he does not exist, and we must live our lives accordingly. When you buy a ticket in a $300 million lottery, there is a very thin possibility, an abstract possibility, that you will win; but the overwhelming odds are you won't. Therefore a reasonable person, while waiting for the lottery drawing, presumes that he will not win; accordingly, he does not quit his job and go shopping for a big house and big yacht. When it comes to winning the lottery, in other words, the reasonable person, though nominally "agnostic," is practically speaking an "atheist." In the United States today almost all who call themselves agnostics are, practically speaking, atheists. The distinction between atheism and agnosticism is a distinction with hardly a difference. The only real difference is this. If you call yourself an atheist, you sound like you have a chip on your shoulder; if you call yourself an agnostic, you sound much more polite.

2. Anti-Christianity. Today's secularists are anti-Christians. When I say this I am not thinking that they are anti-Christian in the sense of being ready to practice discrimination against Christians as individuals. A prejudice (by which I mean a hostile or contemptuous *feeling*) against old-fashioned Christians (e.g., orthodox Catholics and Evangelical Protestants) is fairly widespread among secularists and their liberal Christian fellow-travelers, as can be seen from the mockery often directed by secularists at Christians and from the applause, laughter, and other signs of approval that often greet this mockery.[34] But this is a mild prejudice when compared, for example, with the prejudice white Americans, especially white Southerners, used to direct at black Americans. As for discrimination (by which I mean hostile *behavior*) against traditional Christians, it is rare, except perhaps for hiring and promotion decisions made in the liberal arts and social sciences departments of certain colleges and universities, where secularist professors, who often make up a majority of the screening/hiring committees, are sometimes (maybe often) willing to blackball conspicuously Christian candidates.

---

[34] Watch, for example, Bill Maher's HBO television program.

When I speak of secularists as anti-Christian, what I mean is that they are anti-Christianity. They think Christianity is not only false but dangerous. If they only rarely hope for Christianity to disappear from the world entirely (an attractive but unrealistic hope), they do hope that it will shrink in prominence and influence. The United States as a whole, they feel, would be a better place if we had less Christianity, or if the Christianity we have were to become far less "fundamentalist" and far more liberal or progressive. Moreover, it is believed by secularists that individuals are generally better off when they abandon old-fashioned Christianity and become liberal Christians, and that they are better off still when they abandon Christianity altogether and become secularists; far better off intellectually, and usually better off morally.

This anti-Christianity is a subclass of secularism's hostility to religion in general. If American secularists are more hostile to Christianity than to other religions, this is because Christianity, and not some other religion, has always had, and still has, great prominence and influence in American society and culture. If the United States were a predominantly Hindu nation, American secularists would be especially anti-Hinduism; and if the nation were predominantly Buddhist, they would be especially anti-Buddhism. It happens to be a predominantly Christian nation, and therefore secularists are especially anti-Christianity.

Certain common American religious groups, however, if not exactly treated with respect, are handled with kid gloves. There are four such groups.

(a) Liberal religion. Liberal religion can be found in Protestant, Catholic, and Jewish varieties. A religion becomes liberal (in the sense of the word I have in mind) when, in order to "modernize" itself and keep in step with cultural "progress," it abandons certain of its traditional beliefs, values, and rituals; and the more it abandons these, the more liberal it becomes. In practice, this usually means that liberal religion attempts to accommodate to the prevailing secularism of the day. As I have said above, liberal religion is a kind of halfway house on the road between traditional Christianity (or Judaism) and outright non-religion. This being so, secularism has no great need to denounce liberal religion; for liberal religion has embraced many of the beliefs and values of secularism, and it is from the children and grandchildren of liberal religionists that secularism will recruit the next generation of secularists.

(b) African-American churches. Secularists are generally liberal on matters of race (just as they tend to be liberal on all political issues). That is to say, they deplore the racial injustice that has been so prominent a factor in US history, an injustice that continues (so liberals hold) in many ways to this day. Secularists, like political liberals generally, see themselves as the special friends and protectors of American blacks. They regard themselves (to use an old-fashioned word) as Negrophiles. But since the Christian religion is an important element in black culture, secularists feel they have to go easy on African-American Christianity; they have to cut blacks some slack when it comes to religion. Sometimes, in a spirit of racial condescension (and this is consistent with the spirit of condescension that informs much of political liberalism's attitude toward African-Americans), secularists even look with sympathy on African-American Christianity as a charming "folk religion"—a religion which, though totally absurd in itself and totally unsuitable for a truly rational person, is good enough for black folks.

(c) Judaism. Secularists also go easy on Judaism, but for very different reasons. One of the reasons for this is that many secularists are themselves Jews—that is, non-religious Jews;[35] and while these thoroughly secularized Jews may have little or no use for any kind of religion, they have a kind of nostalgic sympathy for the religion of their parents, grandparents, and ancestors. They don't like to see their fellow secularists direct their religious criticism and mockery specifically at Judaism. Besides, disaffiliating from the Jewish religious community is not an easy thing to do. If you are born a Jew you continue to be a Jew, even if you turn atheist. You become a non-Jew only by

---

[35] In absolute numbers, secularists of Christian ancestry greatly outnumber secularists of Jewish ancestry, but the ratio of "Jewish" secularists to the total Jewish population of the United States is very probably greater than the ratio of "Christian" secularists to the total Christian population. Jews of all varieties (Hasidic, Orthodox, Conservative, Reform, non-religious, and anti-religious) make up a little less than 2 percent of the US population.

specifically renouncing your Jewish identity, and the usual way of doing this is by becoming a member of a non-Jewish religion. Hence attacks on Judaism are attacks on *your* religion—even if you're an atheist. Another reason secularists go easy on Judaism is that those Jews who remain religious are most of them religious in a "liberal" way—that is, they are members of (moderately liberal) Conservative synagogues or (very liberal) Reform synagogues. As we have just seen, there is little reason for secularists to get annoyed at any liberal religion, including liberal Judaism. Secularists, however, even go easy on the "fundamentalist" branch of Judaism, i.e., Orthodox Judaism. Privately the secularist (even the Jewish secularist) believes that Orthodox Judaism is utterly preposterous; but he is reluctant to say this publicly, since any attack on Judaism, even Orthodox Judaism, inevitably carries with it an aroma of anti-Semitism, and for the typical American secularist being anti-Semitic is just as bad as being anti-black. Besides, Orthodox Jews have traditionally stood in a relation of enmity to Christianity, which means that Orthodox Judaism can be tolerated by anti-Christian secularists on the principle of "the enemy of my enemy is my friend."

(d) Islam. If pressed, the secularist would probably say that Islam is so bad that it is even worse than Christianity. However, there are three circumstances that tend to mitigate this harsh judgment. For one, Islam is a traditional foe of Christianity, and here again "the enemy of my enemy" principle goes to work. For another, Muslims in the United States today are often the victims of prejudice coming from conservative Christians and are therefore deserving of secularist sympathy—for secularists are nothing if not enemies of prejudice, especially prejudice emanating from conservative Christians. Finally, the growing presence of Muslims in America makes the United States an increasingly "multicultural" society—and secularists generally like the idea of multiculturalism.

3. Skepticism. Present-day American secularists hold skeptical theories of knowledge—skeptical at all events with regard to certain essential knowledge-claims made by Catholics and other old-fashioned Christians. I say "skeptical theories" (in the plural) because it cannot be said that all secularists are in *positive* agreement on a theory of knowledge; they hold a variety of theories. But they are in *negative* agreement; that is, they agree that the Catholic theory of knowledge is wrong. Let us look at some varieties of secularist skepticism.

(a) No Divine Revelation. Since present-day secularists[36] by definition don't believe in God, they can hardly believe in Divine Revelation. Thus the Bible, from their point of view, while some sections of it may be fine, or at least very significant, "literature," cannot be the word of God. And when Catholicism adds that Tradition is another source of Revelation, this too secularism rejects; Catholic Tradition has not even the merit of being good literature. It goes without saying that secularism, for the same reason that it rejects Scripture and Tradition as sources of Revelation, also rejects revelations putatively made from God to private individuals: that is, the guidance of the Holy Spirit that Christians often claim to have received; not to mention the semi-public Marian apparitions (e.g., La Sallette, Lourdes, Fatima) that official Catholicism has often taken very seriously.

(b) Sensism (also called empiricism). Most secularists hold that human knowledge is limited to sense knowledge, that is, knowledge based on sense experience, whether outer experience obtained by means of the five external senses or experience of our thoughts and feelings obtained by means of an "inner sense." They don't mean that we have to rely on our naked senses alone; it's fine to aid our senses by means of telescopes, microscopes, and other information-enhancing instruments. Nor do they mean to deny our right to make inferences from sense experience to the existence and operation of entities that cannot be directly observed, e.g., subatomic particles or black holes. Further, these sensists/empiricists consider *theoretical* knowledge to be genuine provided it is solidly grounded on sense experience. Take, for instance, Newton's theory of universal gravitation. Nobody can in one glance *observe* the universe as conceived of by Newton, the way one can observe in a single glance, say, a robin sitting on a branch or an apple falling from a tree.

---

[36]   I stress "present-day" here, for in the history of secularism there have been some secularists who have believed in God. In saying this I have in mind Christianity-hating Deists of the 18th and 19th centuries.

But the Newtonian picture of the universe is ultimately based on, and justified by, a vast number of single-glance observations.

If all knowledge is in the last analysis sense knowledge, then it follows that we cannot have any direct knowledge of God or of anything else that is conceived of as non-material (immortal souls, for instance). Nor will secularist sensists/empiricists admit that we can have indirect or inferential knowledge of God or other non-material entities. When sensists allow that we can have inferential knowledge of entities beyond the range of direct experience (subatomic particles, for instance), they conceive of these entities as very, very tiny material things, that is, things having sense characteristics, even though we humans, because of the grossness of our sense organs and the weakness of our instruments, are not able to sense them (at least not to date). If our senses were sufficiently fine or our instruments sufficiently powerful, we *would* be able to observe these entities. Yet no matter how powerful our instruments or how fine our senses, we would never be able to observe God or immortal souls, for they have no sense characteristics. And since only those things are knowable that are, at least in principle, observable, then there can never be any knowledge of God or of immaterial angelic beings or of immortal spiritual souls—not even if such things actually exist.

(c) Moral subjectivism, radical or moderate. Many secularists—*though not all*—insist that moral values, unlike material facts, have no objective existence. If we hold, such secularists tell us, that A is right and B is wrong, or that X is good and Y is bad, this is not because they *are* good/ bad or right/ wrong in themselves. Moral value is subjective;[37] that is, it is a human creation (or "construction," to use today's preferred term). As Hamlet said: "Nothing's either good or bad but thinking makes it so."

Secularists who hold the idea that all moral values are merely subjective have two arguments they use to justify this idea, one negative and one positive. The *negative argument* is based on the theory we just looked at, sensism or

---

[37]   Those who hold this subjectivist view of moral value will usually hold an equally subjectivist view of aesthetic value. Beauty, they contend, is in the eye of the beholder.

empiricism. If sense qualities are all we humans can know, then we cannot know goodness or badness or rightness or wrongness,[38] since none of these has any sense qualities. If I say, "Murder is bloody," this is a sense-testable statement, since blood has sense qualities. But if I say, "Murder is wrong," what is the sense basis for such a statement? How could such a statement be tested by sense observation? What color is wrongness? What does it sound like? What does it taste like? What does it smell like? What does it feel like to the touch? How much does it weigh? To say that murder is bloody is to talk about something objective; to say that it is wrong is to talk about something subjective. The bloodiness is really there, regardless of the opinions of the observer. The wrongness is something the observer adds to the objective situation.[39]

But if sensism shows that moral values cannot be objective, how are we to explain the fact that everybody makes moral valuations, that everybody— including thoroughgoing empiricists—constantly talks in terms of right/wrong and good/bad? This brings us to the second argument, the *positive argument*, that secularists use to justify their moral subjectivism. Moral values, it is held, are "conventions," that is, cultural creations. We know this, secularists contend, from anthropology and sociology. As children we are socialized into a certain culture; and in this process we are taught the language, the customs, and the moral values of that culture. If the socialization process has been even moderately effective, we embrace those cultural values as our personal values. If I grow up in a cannibal culture, I will believe that eating human flesh under certain conditions is morally permissible, even morally obligatory. And if I grow up in the United States, I believe that almost nothing could be more horribly wicked than eating human flesh. It all depends on where I happen to grow up. Moral values (say many secularists) are social creations; they are not facts that exist independently of the wishes of society. The moon and the

---

[38] Or beauty or ugliness.

[39] That a subjectivist theory of morality follows logically from strict empiricism can be seen most clearly in the writings of the Logical Positivists. See, for instance, the classic English work on Logical Positivism, A. J. Ayer's *Language, Truth and Logic*, chapter 6, "Critique of Ethics and Theology."

Rock of Gibraltar and polar bears in the Arctic exist independently of anyone's wishes, but moral values don't exist that way. That's explains why all societies, including both cannibals and Americans, agree that the moon exists while they disagree about the rightness or wrongness of eating human flesh.

An increasingly popular deviation from this "social convention" idea of moral values is what may be called the "personal choice" idea. According to this, the moral values that an individual lives by are not—or at least *should* not be—imposed on the individual by society; rather they are values that the individual has adopted for himself/herself. I say this is becoming "increasingly popular," and there are two reasons for this. First, in a society like the United States in which the belief in personal freedom is becoming stronger and stronger, it occurs to many people, especially young people, to ask: "By what right does society impose *its* values on me? If I have rejected the values of my parents and teachers and the pope, why can't I also, if I wish, reject the values of American society?" And they answer this question by saying, "I'll choose, or even create, my own values. If I wish to embrace popular American values, I can do that. And if I wish to reject them and substitute something else, I can do that too." Second, we live in a society in which, more and more, there is great disagreement about moral values— values having to do with sexual freedom, homosexuality, abortion, suicide, the use of recreational drugs, and a hundred other things; and so society, not having any common values to impose on its members, forces individuals to choose for themselves.

In any case, whether it's a matter of empiricism or social convention or personal choice or two or three of these combined, secularists are in general subjectivists on the question of moral values. That is to say, they are *deniers* when it comes to the objectivity of moral values.

However, I said at the beginning of this subsection that *not all* secularists hold this position of what may be called "radical moral subjectivism." For if *all* values were purely subjective, how would secularists be able to condemn—as they do, often in very strenuous terms—the wickedness of Christian conservatives who make efforts to ban, say, abortion and same-sex marriage? And so we find that many contemporary American secularists, probably the great majority of them, hold a view we may call "moderate moral subjectivism," a view that is a blend (an incoherent blend, to be sure) of moral objectivism and moral subjectivism. On the one hand they hold that there is a real difference, an objective difference, between moral and immoral conduct. Conduct is immoral, they say, when it harms another person, and it is morally permissible when it does not. On the other hand, all other moral values are simply subjective preferences—either personal preferences or preferences instilled in a person by the socialization process of his/her society. For instance, rape is objectively immoral because it causes harm to an unwilling person, but gay sex between two consenting adults is not wrong because it causes no harm; and if you (a Catholic, let's say) happen to think that gay sex is wrong, this is nothing but your subjective opinion, an opinion derived either from your Catholic education or from your personal prejudice. This moderate moral subjectivism is obviously inconsistent with the sensism/empiricism I described in the preceding subsection. For if you are a consistent sensist, you ought to deny the objectivity of *all* moral values[40] and moral rules; you ought to hold, for instance, that wife-beating is not objectively wrong; when we say it's wrong all we mean is that our society disapproves of it or that we personally disapprove of it.

How can secularists, who reject that idea that there is such a thing as moral *knowledge*, contend that there are some moral judgments that have universal validity? The typical secularist would hold, for instance, that such anti-female practices as genital mutilation, wife-beating, rape, and child marriage are always and everywhere morally wrong, even if this or that local culture says that they are right. It is easy for Catholics to condemn these activities as morally wrong, holding as they do that there is an unchanging and universal unwritten moral law (Natural Law) and that we have knowledge of this law. But how can a secularist, who, consistent with his empiricism/sensism, denies the existence of moral knowledge, condemn these activities in an unequivocal way?

---

[40]   You also ought to deny the objectivity of aesthetic values. You ought to reject the idea that, say, the music of Mozart or Beethoven is truly superior to the music of the latest popular hip-hop artist.

The answer, I suggest, is this. If moral judgments cannot be based on knowledge, it follows that they must be based on feeling; for there is no third possibility.[41] Is there, then, a universal feeling that leads everyone—everyone, that is, who is emotionally normal—to condemn anti-female violence and certain other kinds of wrong-doing? The answer to this question, an answer almost universally embraced by present-day American secularists, is that there is indeed such a universal feeling, namely compassion. It is compassion that leads us to condemn all conduct and all laws and all customs and all institutions that do harm to others. Let compassion be your great moral guide in life; and even though there is no such thing as moral knowledge, you will condemn all injustice that comes to your attention, for you will feel pity for the victims of this injustice. And thus you will condemn rape and wife-beating and female genital mutilation and all customs that treat girls and women as second-class human beings. And you will condemn racism, which inflicts pain and suffering on blacks and other ethnic minorities. And you will condemn opposition to same-sex marriage, which causes pain to gays and lesbians. And you will condemn laws that prohibit abortion, for such laws cause pain to women who are pregnant with unwanted babies.

But, somebody may ask, what about these unborn babies? Shouldn't we feel compassion for them? Shouldn't we therefore condemn abortion? "Well," the logically consistent secularist will say, "if we actually did feel compassion then we'd have to condemn abortion in those cases in which our compassion for the baby outweighed compassion for the pregnant woman/girl who wishes to abort. But in fact nobody—at least almost nobody—actually feels compassion for the unborn baby/fetus. Even prolife people, except in rare instances, have no feelings of pity for the baby. They are convinced that a great injustice is being done to the unborn baby; but they don't have true

---

41   This helps to explain, by the way, why secularists insist that opposition to homosexuality and same-sex marriage is based on homophobia, hatred of gay persons. If opposition to homosexuality or SSM is not based on knowledge (for no moral judgments are based on knowledge), then it must be based on feeling; and what feeling is most likely to lead to a condemnation of homosexuality and SSM? Why, homophobia of course.

feelings of pity for the entity being aborted. Nature seems to have made us humans in such a way that, while we have a great capacity for pity, we are unable to feel that pity for unborn babies. And so in practice it's easy to make the abortion call: pity for the pregnant woman/girl is always stronger than the non-pity or very-weak-pity that the normal human being feels for the unborn baby. Therefore," the secularist concludes, "abortion is never wrong."

(d) Constructivism. For a few decades now many *au courant* academic secularists have contended that theories about reality are often, if not always, "social constructions." That is, these theories are not solidly based on reality itself; they don't give an accurate picture of the world as it really is. Instead they are based on the class, gender, racial, and economic interests of those who create and embrace and promote the theories. In effect, theories of reality are philosophical or scientific *fictions*. When these theories find a large and receptive audience, this is because of three co-operating agencies: those (a small number) who manufacture the fictions, those (a larger number) who attempt to "sell" the fictions to the broader public, and those (a very large number) who are deluded into accepting the fiction as a true report of reality.

Academics who hold this "social construction" idea are usually found in college and university departments of behavioral science or humanities or in law schools; rarely are they found in departments of science and engineering. Why? Because it is difficult for scientists and engineers, accustomed as they are to the scientific method and familiar with the evidence that underlies broadly accepted scientific theories, to convince themselves that these theories are *not* based on reality, that they do *not* give a more or less accurate picture of the world of nature as it really is. By contrast, it is not especially difficult for scholarly students of philosophy, literature, history, sociology, psychology, law, etc. to convince themselves that widely held theories about the subject-matter of their disciplines are something other than accurate pictures of reality.

The intellectual roots of this constructivism go back to Karl Marx and his work *The German Ideology* (co-authored with Friedrich Engels in 1846). Marx did not invent the word "ideology," but he gave it a meaning that has pretty much stuck to it ever since. An ideology, as Marx saw it, is a systematic interpretation of reality, or some aspect of reality, that serves to defend and justify the social, economic, and political interests of some social class, usually society's ruling class. Thus the modern "science" of (non-Marxian) economics served to protect the interests of the capitalist class. And depending on the particular society and its state of historical development, the "science" of theology, flexible in its servitude, has justified the interests of the old ruling class (the landed aristocracy) or the new ruling class (the capitalists). Neither does theology give an accurate picture of the universe, nor does economics give an accurate picture of the economic life of modern society. Both give fictional pictures that tend to justify and defend the status quo. The same is true, according to Marx, of all other branches of social science and philosophy.

When our present-day academics talk about "constructions" of reality, they are usually speaking as heirs of Marx.[42] Unlike Marx himself, however, they are not exclusively concerned with the class struggle (though that's one of their concerns). They have in mind other social struggles as well—for instance, struggles between men and women; between whites and non-whites; between straights and gays; between rich countries (above all the United States) and poor countries; between globalist corporations and the wretched of the earth; and so on. Ideologies have been constructed by men to keep women subordinate, by whites to keep "persons of color" in their place, by straights to justify their scapegoating of gays, by rich countries to justify their oppression of poor countries, by globalists to justify their exploitation of the poorest people on the planet, etc. So when you come across a widely-held and widely-propagated theory, you needn't ask, "Is it true?" Of course it isn't true. What you should ask is, "What special interest is this theory designed to protect?"

4. Naturalism. When it comes to metaphysics, secularism offers naturalism as a replacement for belief in a supernatural realm of being, including God and the afterlife. By naturalism I mean the idea that the world of nature is all there is, that there is nothing beyond or above or outside nature. It is hard to believe that

---

[42]   It has often been observed that Marxism, having been discredited by the many disastrous Communist experiments of the 20th century, survives today only among professors at universities located in capitalist countries.

naturalism will ever prove satisfactory to the majority of Americans in the long run. It is a bleak view of reality, and while it satisfies a certain respectable class of minds, such minds are, and probably always will be, few and far between. Perhaps this explains why secularists generally don't promote naturalism with great enthusiasm and noise; they realize they have a weak candidate. Or is it because they feel that the best way to make naturalism prevail in the world is by injecting it quietly, very quietly, into a nation's cultural bloodstream?

In practice, the form of naturalism most commonly embraced by American secularists is materialism; that is, the theory that everything in existence is either material or a function of that which is material, there being no non-material or spiritual realm of being. However, more sophisticated naturalists—I have in mind those who have had a philosophical education and as a result cannot help but feel that materialism is philosophically indefensible—don't insist on materialism. They do no more than insist on naturalism. Materialism makes a *positive* statement about the nature of reality, saying that it is entirely made up of matter; naturalism on the other hand is content to make a *negative* statement, namely, that there is nothing beyond nature. Out of respect for these philosophical and more cautious naturalists, I will here refer to secularism's metaphysical theory as naturalism, not materialism—even though, as I said, most secularist naturalists are in fact materialists.

In any case, their commitment to naturalism is demonstrated by the agitated reaction of secularists whenever somebody challenges the Darwinian theory of evolution,[43] even when—or perhaps I should say especially when—this challenge comes, not from Biblical literalists who want to uphold the idea of a six-day creation, but from persons with doctorates who accept the principle of evolution yet contend that a Darwinian theory is unable to account for all the facts that have accompanied evolution. Even those secularists (no doubt the

---

[43]   When I say "the Darwinian theory of evolution" I may seem to be suggesting that there is only one such theory. But in fact there are numerous "Darwinian" theories. What they all hold in common, however, is Charles Darwin's thesis that biological evolution has taken place as a result of two leading factors: random mutation and natural selection. I am calling "Darwinian," then, all theories of biological evolution that hinge on random mutation and natural selection.

great majority) who are very close to being biological illiterates feel compelled to jump to the defense of the Darwinian version and to denounce—and not just denounce, but denounce with scorn and indignation—the critics, without of course having studied the criticisms with any care. Why is this? Because they have a gut feeling that the future of naturalism is linked to the future of Darwinism: if Darwinism goes down, they fear, so will naturalism.

Now, there is no logical or essential connection between Darwinism and naturalism. As a biologist, you can be a Darwinian without being a naturalist; and as a philosopher, you can be a naturalist without being a Darwinian. Historically, however, the two have been linked. Early on, naturalists seized on the new Darwinian theory (1859 was the year of publication of Darwin's *The Origin of Species*) as substantial evidence that naturalism/materialism is true and that God doesn't exist—or in any case that God is an unnecessary hypothesis. Fallacious as this linkage is, it nonetheless continues to have a hold on most naturalist/secularist minds. Conversely and ironically, the linkage also continues to have a hold on the minds of many conservative religious believers. And so believers and naturalists reinforce one another's false belief in the linkage, the former feeling that they must destroy Darwinism in order to protect their religion, while the latter feel that they must defend Darwinism if they wish to preserve naturalism.

Catholic thought distinguishes between (a) scientific theories of evolution (whether they be Darwinian or non-Darwinian) and (b) the metaphysical theory of naturalism. Catholicism has no objection to a scientifically well-founded theory of evolution, but it objects strongly to a metaphysical theory of naturalism—since naturalism is tantamount to atheism. Catholicism will therefore object to any theory of *naturalistic* evolution, that is, any hybrid theory that combines evolutionary science with metaphysical naturalism. Many secularists who claim to be "defenders" of the scientific theory of evolution against its "anti-scientific" religious enemies are actually, whether they realize it or not, defenders of a theory that is not scientific at all, namely, this hybrid scientific-philosophical theory of naturalistic evolutionism.

It should be noted that the naturalist believes not only in the "small" evolution of life on a single very small planet, Earth, but also in the "big" evolution of the cosmos.[44] If a divine creator of the universe doesn't exist, then the universe must have evolved accidentally; that is to say, cosmic evolution must have taken place. Biological evolution on Earth does nothing of course to prove that cosmic evolution took place and is still taking place. But in the imagination of secularists/naturalists, there is a strong association between the two kinds of evolution, and there is a feeling—not a very logical feeling, but a strong feeling nonetheless—that if naturalistic biological evolution fails, so will cosmic evolution. Thus it is not surprising to find secularists/naturalists fighting fiercely to defend biological evolution and a naturalistic understanding thereof.

5. Moral Liberalism. If you wish to replace Christianity and offer something positive in its place, you will have to replace the Christian code of morality with a new code, a "new morality." Hence secularism has given us the morality of *moral liberalism*. If secularists have been relatively low-key about their naturalism ("injecting it quietly, very quietly, into a nation's cultural bloodstream"), they are quite the opposite when it comes to their moral liberalism. This they shout from the rooftops, everywhere urging its great merits and brow-beating those who don't agree.

Moral liberalism, as I said earlier, is composed of two complementary principles, the Personal Liberty Principle (PLP) and the Tolerance Principle (TP). To repeat what I've already said: according to the PLP, a person is morally free to do whatever he or she would like to do provided this conduct does no harm to others; and according to the TP, which is simply the other side of the same coin, we have a moral duty to respect the right of others to do whatever they wish provided their conduct does no harm to others. Reduced to specifics, the theory of moral liberalism is used to justify a number of activities condemned by traditional Christian morality: fornication, unmarried cohabitation, out-of-wedlock childbirth, abortion, homosexuality, bisexuality, same-sex marriage, pornography, sadomasochism, suicide, physician-assisted suicide, euthanasia, recreational drug use, etc.

---

[44] Darwin himself had nothing to do with cosmic evolution. It was his contemporary, Herbert Spencer (1820-1903) who popularized the idea of cosmic evolution. Even though nobody reads Spencer anymore, it might be said that today's secularists are Spencerians more than they are Darwinians.

In practice, however, a number of qualifications have to be attached to the PLP and TP if we are to understand the real content of moral liberalism.

- Harm to others renders an act immoral only if the "other" is a non-consenting other. If Jones is harmed by Smith as the direct result of a consensual act that Smith performs on Jones (let's say a sado-masochistic act) Smith cannot be blamed.
- The "harm" in question has to be harm in the temporal/material order; that is, harm that is material, financial, psychological, or reputational, not harm that is purely spiritual. Thus it doesn't count as harm if the conduct impairs a person's relationship with God, or damages a person's purity of soul, or diminishes a person's chances of a happy afterlife.
- Normally the harm in question has to produce pain or suffering in the victim. I say "normally" because it is possible, though exceedingly rare, that I might harm him without causing any pain or suffering; e.g., if I were to steal ten dollars from a multi-billionaire it is unlikely that the victim of this theft would experience any pain or suffering.
- The harm in question has to be obvious. It can be argued with some plausibility, for instance, that the legalization of same-sex marriage will, after a few decades, impair the institution of marriage and thereby jeopardize the well-being of millions of children—but since the truth of this is far from "obvious," the argument doesn't count against same-sex marriage.
- Doing harm to another while engaged in an act of self-defense is permissible.
- Likewise society in general is permitted to harm criminals in order to discourage criminals from harming society. This harming of criminals, however, should not extend to the death penalty; for if the aim of penalties is to prevent or deter future crime, this can be secured just as well by a long prison sentence.
- Finally, there is the difficult problem of abortion. Moral liberals very much wish to say that abortion is morally permissible. Indeed the freedom to abort is the keystone of their system of sexual freedom; for if abortion is not available as a "safety net," a regime of sexual

freedom becomes thoroughly impractical. At the same time it seems obvious that abortion does harm—nothing less than lethal harm—to the unborn baby who gets aborted. So how does moral liberalism deal with this problem? This is done in one or more of eight ways (all of which, as can easily be seen, are intellectually dishonest—for all of them try to evade the fact of the humanity of the unborn baby):

1) By denying that the aborted entity is a human being.

2) By denying that the aborted baby experiences any pain or suffering.

3) By defining the abortion as a kind of mercy killing, i.e., killing the unborn child for the sake of its own well-being.

4) By focusing so heavily on the sad situation of the woman/girl having the abortion that the sad situation of the unborn baby comes to seem a thing of no real significance.

5) By regarding abortion as part and parcel of a progressive sexual morality, at the same time holding a tacit theory that all "progress" is good. Therefore it is quite unnecessary to spend time worrying over the possibility that an injustice is done to the unborn baby.

6) Personal liberty is an absolute and indubitable good, while the humanity of the fetus/baby is a doubtful thing; therefore we don't have to concern ourselves about the latter.

7) We just don't know whether the entity being aborted is human or not. Therefore it's okay to kill it.

8) Moral-religious conservatives who object to abortion are in general less well-educated and less prosperous than we prochoice people; whenever there is a moral conflict between them and us, a reasonable person will presume that we are right and they are wrong.

In fairness to moral liberals, it should be noted that there is more to their moral philosophy than this merely permissive rule (that is, that you are free to do what you like provided you don't harm others). That expresses the *negative* side of their morality: thou shalt do no harm to others. There is also, however, a *positive* side to their moral theory. In addition to doing no harm to others, you should try to help them. In a minimal way, of course, you help them by minding your own business, by keeping out of their way, by tolerating their behavior; this is the TP spoken of above. But there are thousands of more positive ways of helping others. For instance, you can become a teacher in an inner-city school, or an underpaid nurse at a clinic for poor people, or an abortionist at a Planned Parenthood clinic, or an environmental scientist, or a social worker, or a public defender working for poverty-stricken clients, or an animal rights activist, or a volunteer lawyer for the ACLU, or a Peace Corps volunteer, or a lobbyist for a worthy cause at city hall or the state capitol; and so on and so forth. Such activities, however, while considered by the moral liberal to be ethically admirable, are not strict duties. Other things being equal, the person who engages in these "helping" activities is an ethically more admirable person that the person who does no more than abstain from harming others. But the latter person is without moral guilt. Another way of putting this is to say that there are two kinds of morality, a morality of strict duty and a morality of aspiration.[45] From the point of view of moral liberalism the "do no harm" rule belongs to the morality of strict duty, while the "help others" rule belongs to the morality of aspiration.

The Enemy Within

And there you have it, my dear bishops: a portrait of the enemy, the enemy of the Catholic religion—which religion, if it is not rude of me to remind you, is the religion of which you are supposed to be the custodians. Unlike some earlier anti-Christianity enemies (I have in mind Nazis and Communists) the present American enemies are not *vicious* enemies. They are not sadists, they don't lust for blood (except, one might say, for the blood of unborn babies), they have no wish to create Christian martyrs, and they have no totalitarian

---

[45] For a famous formulation of this distinction, see Henri Bergson's work, *The Two Sources of Morality and Religion*—a work which, however, offers scant support for moral liberalism.

aspirations (although they perhaps have totalitarian tendencies). Our enemies are almost all of them people of upper-middle class status, or at least people who (while they may at the moment be occupying lower-middle class positions) realistically aspire to upper-middle class status; our enemies are cultured and well-educated; they read the latest high-quality novels and biographies; they see the best movies and listen to good music; they have good taste and good manners; they drink good coffee and good wine, and they eat at good restaurants. Nonetheless they are anti-Christian, profoundly so. Of all the modern enemies of Catholicism they are the most dangerous. For they proceed, not by means of coercion and terror, but by means of persuasion and seduction. They don't *drive* people away from Christianity, they *lure* them away.

You, my dear bishops, have the duty of leading the fight against this enemy; for if *you* don't lead, who will? A leaderless Catholic community will never be able to withstand such a powerful and seductive foe. Yet, as I have said again and again in the course of this book, you have done a poor job of leading the fight during the last 40 years or so. Why is this? *Because of the enemy within.* You have not done an effective job of fighting the enemy without because you have been ineffective at fighting the enemy within.

Who is this "enemy within"? It is those who wish to "modernize" the Church and bring it "up to date." When I say this, an important verbal clarification is needed. For there are two kinds of Catholic "modernizers," one of whom is a religious liberal (i.e., a Catholic who wishes to water down Catholic doctrine and morality in order to accommodate it to the secular world) and the other not. In other words, one is illegitimate, the other legitimate; and the two are often confused with one another. Let's say you're the kind of Catholic modernizer who would like your pastor to create a webpage for the parish; or you want the pastor of your parish to consult the laity when formulating a parish agenda; or you'd like to see the Vatican lend its support to the democratic transformation of Third World authoritarian regimes; or you want Catholicism to recognize that we all have a moral duty to protect the physical environment; or you want Catholic higher education to involve a familiarity with (though not necessarily an approval of) the latest fashions in philosophical thought and literary criticism; or you want Catholicism to be strongly committed to discovering non-military ways of solving international problems; or you'd like to see women occupy important and powerful posts in the Church's bureaucracy; or you insist that no Catholic priest, nun, or layperson should be punished by the Church without due process, including the right to confront his/her accusers; or (to take an extravagant hypothetical) you argue that the Vatican should auction off its immensely valuable art collections and use the proceeds to provide potable water for poor people living in Third World shantytowns. In all these cases you'd be a certain kind of modernizer, but you would *not* be a religious liberal (or "progressive"); that is, you would not be calling on Catholicism to abandon or to amend any of the essentials of its doctrine, morality, ritual, or government. But if you said that Jesus, while a very wise and very virtuous man, was not God; or that the Eucharist, while a wonderful symbol, is not truly the body and blood of Christ; or that abortion or homosexual conduct or adultery or fornication are not sinful; or that the Mass can be celebrated by a person other than a priest; or that the office of bishop can be done away with; or that the pope is not infallible; or that women should be ordained priests—if you say any of these things, then you *are* a religious liberal, you are a Catholic modernizer of the illegitimate kind.

Some liberal Catholics are consciously and actively liberal: they are quite deliberately working to transform Catholicism's nature. Most, however, are liberal in an unwitting and passive way: they don't so much have a liberal philosophy as they have liberal sentiments; while not actively working to change the religion in a modernist direction, they would not resist such changes; in many cases they would welcome them. In the American Catholic Church today, there is a far greater number of passive than of active liberals. Without the quiet consent and encouragement of passive liberals, active liberals would have little motive to keep up their struggle, and would have little influence.

You bishops have generally been unwilling to "take on" these religious liberals, whether active or passive, and resist their agenda. Perhaps this is because you fear their numbers. After all, they make up a great portion of the Catholic laity, perhaps even a majority. And so I can imagine how you might defend your inaction: "If we antagonize them," you'll say, "we may drive them out of the Church; and driving them out, we will have driven out their children, grandchildren, great-grandchildren, etc. These generations will be lost to the Church; and of at least equal if not more importance, the Church will be lost to them. Better, then, to abide the liberals for the present, and someday, perhaps a long time from now, they or their descendants will return to authentic Catholicism. The job of a bishop is to preach the Gospel, yes; but it is also, let me remind you, a bishop's job to hold the Church together. When preaching the Gospel threatens to destroy the Church, a bishop is faced with a grave dilemma. Should he preach the Gospel, or should he preserve the Church? It is unfair of you, a mere layman with no governing responsibility, to denounce a bishop because, faced with this dilemma, he opts to keep the Church from going to pieces."

As an abstract matter, I grant all this. But it is odd that the great majority of you bishops have opted to grasp the "let's hold the Church together" horn of the dilemma instead of the "let's preach the Gospel" horn. As a result you have left the Gospel relatively unpreached when it comes to matters like sexual freedom, abortion, and same-sex marriage. The trouble with your strategy is not that it's a strategy no honest bishop could try. No, the trouble is that *it has not worked*. For forty years it has been tried and found wanting. The Gospel is unpreached *and* the Church is falling apart.

If you have been unwilling to confront the semi-secularism of the liberal Catholic, it is not at all surprising that you have been ineffective at confronting the full-blown secularism of the secularist himself. The road to recovery, then, involves preaching the Gospel—that is to say, preaching the Catholic religion: preaching it first of all to Catholics, and then to the world at large. This will not, I grant, be easy to do; for Catholicism, from the point of view of the typical modern mind (including the nominally Catholic modern mind), is a strange religion, a *very* strange religion—indeed an absurd religion.[46] It will take courage on your part to preach it in its unmitigated form, since doing so will bring down on you the indignation of "progressive" Catholics, who will be backed up by the sneers of outright secularists, including those who dominate the command posts of American culture, namely the mass media,

---

[46] Remember Tetullian's famous remark: "Credo quia absurdum" ("I believe because it is absurd").

the entertainment industry, and our best institutions of higher education. But if your predecessor bishops in Roman times were willing to face lions, surely you can muster the courage needed to withstand indignation and sneers.

Having examined the *nature* of today's anti-Christian secularism in this chapter, in the next two chapters I plan to examine the *history* of American anti-Christian secularism.

[end of chapter]

CHAPTER 5

Five Stages of American Secularism

Anti-Christianity in the United States is today entering a new stage. Since the 1960s anti-Christianity has been in a stage of *practical atheism*, the most striking manifestation of which has been the so-called "sexual revolution." But more recently, with the publication in 2006 and 2007 of a number of best-selling books that are very explicitly anti-Christian, we are, it seems, passing beyond merely tacit and practical atheism to a stage of very overt *theoretical atheism*. I should add that this theoretical atheism, by going "beyond" practical atheism, will not nullify the latter; on the contrary, it will reinforce it, making it even stronger.

In the present chapter I will offer what Hollywood calls a "prequel" to present-day anti-Christianity. I want to take a look—a very condensed look—at the entire history of anti-Christianity in America, a history that can be divided into six stages. In this chapter I'll deal with the first five of these stages, saving the sixth for the next chapter.

First stage: Deism

Colonial America lagged a bit behind the times, and so it was not until the second half of the 18th century that Deism, which had been in vogue in

England in the late 17th and early 18th centuries, struck roots in America. And they weren't very deep roots at that. Not many Americans were Deists; almost all men and women living in the thirteen original colonies/states were Protestants, and even most Deists were nominal Protestants. But among the small Deistic minority there were, as we'll see in a moment, some notable Americans.

Almost all Deists, both in Europe and in America, while differing from one another in many ways, held certain beliefs in common:

- that an almighty and morally perfect Supreme Being—God, as popularly called—exists;
- that God created the world of nature and the laws that govern it;[47]
- that the existence of God can be known from a study of nature and its uniform laws;
- that there are not, and never have been,[48] miracles (for why would God, the all-knowing and all-powerful creator of the world, feel the need to "amend" his creation from time to time?);
- that God is good, and wishes humans—the noblest and most godlike of his creatures—to be happy and good;
- that there is a life after death in which we will be rewarded or punished for our earthly virtues or vices;
- that God—or Nature, God's surrogate—has provided us with a natural capacity for knowing right and wrong;
- that the only worship and honor God wants from us is that we serve him by serving our fellow man;

---

[47] The stupendous achievements of Isaac Newton (who was a Christian, not a Deist, albeit not a perfectly orthodox Christian), especially his law of universal gravitation, strongly impressed upon the European mind and imagination the idea that God works in the world according to uniform laws.

[48] It was nothing new to deny modern-day miracles, since many Protestants, unlike Catholics, generally held that miracles had ceased with the closing of the New Testament era. But to deny *all* miracles, including those reported in the Bible— this was decidedly new.

- that although God has revealed himself through reason or intuition to all humans, he has made no special revelation to any man, to any nation, or to any church—in other words, Judaism, Christianity, and Islam are false insofar as they claim to possess a special revelation from God and, as a result of this imagined revelation, add to the simple and universal religion of Deism.

Deists in America, as in Europe, fell into two categories, extreme anti-Christians and moderate anti-Christians. The most famous extremist in Europe was Voltaire, who hated Christianity in general and Catholicism (the religion of his country, the religion in which he had been brought up) in particular. An example of a moderate anti-Christian was the German philosopher Immanuel Kant. Reared a Pietistic Protestant, Kant drifted away from revealed religion toward what he considered a superior kind of religious thought and practice, yet without denouncing Christianity and while defending an ultra-strict Christian ethic. His mature view was neatly summed up in the title of one of his books, *Religion within the Limits of Reason Alone.*

In America the most famous of the moderate Deists were Benjamin Franklin and Thomas Jefferson. Franklin abandoned the Christianity (in particular, the Calvinism) of his Boston youth, but he made no attacks on the old religion. Just the opposite, he gave financial support to all the churches in Philadelphia.[49] His idea seems to have been that it is important for people to have *some* religion even if it is not the very best; and so, if ordinary people cannot rise to the level of Deism, well, Christianity will have to do as a second best. Jefferson had no use for the miraculous and (in his view) irrational elements in Christianity, but he retained a great admiration for the Founder of the religion: so much so that when he was in the White House he used some of his spare time (presidents were apparently less busy in those days than now) to put together a redacted version of the Gospels, in which he deleted all the "superstitious" elements that had crept into the story of Jesus. What Jefferson produced was in effect a

---

[49] His account of this can be found in his wonderful autobiography, one of the best American books ever written.

95

Deistic biography of Jesus.[50] The book was not published till after Jefferson's death, and in his lifetime Jefferson made no public criticisms of Christianity.

The most famous of the American *extreme* Deists was Tom Paine (that is, if Paine—active in the political life of three nations, America, Britain, and France—can properly be called an American at all). While in prison in France during the Reign of Terror of the 1790s, he wrote *The Age of Reason*, a furiously anti-Christianity diatribe. His anti-Christianity was as intense as that of his predecessor, Voltaire, though without Voltaire's sense of humor. Although previously honored, and justly so, as a great American patriot, Paine saw his American reputation plunge to the depths following publication of this book. For the United States at this time—the late 1700s and early 1800s— was entering an era of great religious revival, the so-called "Second Great Awakening." The nation was in no mood to applaud overt anti-Christians, regardless of their patriotic contributions at the time of the Revolution. One other strongly anti-Christian American Deist was yet another patriot, Ethan Allen, leader of the "Green Mountain Boys" who captured Fort Ticonderoga and dragged its cannons from Lake George to Boston, where they were utilized by George Washington to force the British to evacuate the city. Allen wrote a strongly anti-Christianity book titled, *Reason the Only Oracle of Man*.

Second Stage: Unitarianism

It is with some reluctance that I include Unitarianism as a stage in American anti-Christianity. Why? Because the early Unitarians—for example, William Ellery Channing, the "father" of American Unitarianism[51]—were anything but *intentional* anti-Christians. Quite the contrary, Channing and his

---

[50] See *The Jefferson Bible: the Life and Morals of Jesus of Nazareth* (Beacon Press, 1989).

[51] For Channing's classic statement of the basic beliefs of Unitarianism, see his Baltimore sermon on the occasion of the ordination of Jared Sparks, "Unitarian Christianity" (1819). This sermon was a kind of Unitarian declaration of independence, making clear its separation from Calvinistic Congregationalism.

associates (let's call them first-generation Unitarians) sincerely believed that their version of Christianity was the truest and best version. They felt that they were continuing and completing the work of the Protestant Reformation. The Reformers of the 16th century believed that they were purging Christianity of some of the non-Biblical extras that Rome had added to it. But the Reformers, in the eyes of Unitarians, had not gone far enough. Unitarians would now finish the job of Reformation, deleting all "irrational" elements from Christianity (for example, the Trinity and the Divinity of Christ), and by so doing they would get back to the original religion of Jesus Christ.

In retrospect, it seems preposterous that they could have believed that their highly rationalistic version of Christianity, which suited the prosperous and cultured upper classes of early 19th century Boston, was identical with the religion of Jesus. They seem to have imagined that Jesus was a particularly admirable teacher of the Boston Brahmin type who would have found himself right at home on Beacon Hill. Preposterous or not, however, this is what these good and well-meaning persons honestly believed. So in fairness we should credit them with being Christian by intention even if they were not Christian in fact. But de facto their religion was a kind of anti-Christianity.

Boston Unitarianism was the first form of "liberal Christianity" in the United States, and it did what liberal Christianity has done ever since: that is, it tried to find a middle ground (a *via media*) between traditional Christianity and the secularism or anti-Christianity that happened to be in fashion at the moment. This might almost be given as a definition of liberal Christianity: a well-intentioned but utterly absurd attempt to blend unblendable opposites. In the Unitarian instance, the secularist pole of the antithesis was Deism; hence early Unitarianism was a blend of Christianity and Deism—a reverence for the Bible and Jesus and Christian morality combined with a rejection of the Trinity and the Divinity of Christ." Later forms of liberal Christianity, as we'll see below, attempted to blend Christianity with agnosticism or with an ethic of sexual freedom. But since Christianity and anti-Christianity are opposites, the "blend" of the two will have no coherence, no stability. This is what happened with Unitarianism; it had no stability, the result being that the orthodox Unitarianism of Channing's generation disintegrated in the second generation, that of Ralph Waldo Emerson, Theodore Parker, and their Transcendentalist friends.

Emerson, it can be said in truth, is one of the great figures in the history of American religion and morality—a reminder of the fact that you can be a foe of Christianity while being a religious person with an inspiring moral message; you can be, as Emerson was, a pantheist who calls on us to trust the Godlike core of our being.[52] Be that as it may, Emerson, if we are to take his writings as a true expression of his mind, was not a Christian, not even in an extended sense of the word.[53] (However, it should be noted that throughout his lifetime—which is to say, long after he had abandoned the Christian system of belief and had resigned from the Unitarian ministry—Emerson remained a member of the Unitarian Church, and at the end he was buried from his parish church, the Unitarian church in his hometown of Concord). Within less than a half-century, from the early Channing to the mature Emerson, liberal religion had gone from "purifying" Christianity to the complete abandonment of Christianity in favor of a decidedly non-Christian pantheism.

In the case of Unitarianism, the downhill slide from Christianity to its opposite took place in a shorter time than has been the case with subsequent liberal religions. But all forms of liberal Christianity slide down the same slope. They may not reach the bottom as quickly as did Unitarianism, but they all move in the same direction and will hit bottom sooner or later. It is a kind of ecclesiastical law of gravity. Show me a religion that has embraced religious liberalism, and I'll show you a religion that has embraced a course of gradual suicide.

The same would be true if Catholicism were to transform itself into a liberal religion. It is odd that today's liberal Catholics seem unaware of this. Can it be that they have not taken the trouble to study the history of liberal Protestantism?

---

[52] For Emerson's pantheism, see his essays "Self-Reliance," "The Oversoul," and "Nature." Also look at his poem "The Problem," the best brief summary of his pantheistic ideas.

[53] Of course if you give a completely non-dogmatic meaning to "Christian," and if by "Christian" you simply mean "a good person," then you can call Emerson a Christian—and you can also call Confucius and Socrates Christians. But this is a great abuse of the English language.

Or can it be that they are willing to see their religion destroyed? And what about you bishops? Are you not familiar with the history of liberal religion? Are you not familiar with the history of mainline American Protestantism, in which liberalism has been influential since the early 20th century and has had the upper hand since the 1950s? And if you are familiar with all this, why haven't you been more vigorous in battling against Christianity-destroying liberalism in the Catholic Church?

Third Stage: Agnosticism, Merely Negative Secularism

The first two stages of American anti-Christianity, Deism and Unitarianism, provided theistic alternatives to Christianity; or in the case of Emerson, a pantheistic alternative. It was not until the third stage—I am now speaking of the period between the Civil War and World War I—that an overtly non-theistic form of anti-Christianity emerged. This was *agnosticism*, a new word in the late 19th century, coined by the English biologist and agnostic, Thomas Henry Huxley, a great champion of Darwin and Darwinism.[54] American agnosticism was largely derivative from English agnosticism. In England the leading agnostics were Huxley and the philosopher Herbert Spencer, the latter of whom made a famous distinction between The Knowable (which science can study) and The Unknowable (which religion and myth can fantasize about, if they like). Charles Darwin happened to be an agnostic in the latter part of his life. However, though other agnostics—the kind who, like Huxley, might be called "crusading agnostics" or "apostles of agnosticism"—frequently shouted Darwin's name, Darwin himself was not an apostle of agnosticism; he was content to be a scientist who happened to have lost his personal religious faith.

The agnostic movement had three principal anti-Christianity arguments, one of them epistemological, a second based on Darwinism, and a third based on German Biblical scholarship.

---

[54] Because of the doggedness of his defense of Darwinism, Huxley was given the honorific nickname, "Darwin's bulldog."

---

(1) The epistemological argument purported to be based on science, and it was eagerly embraced by those who were pleased to have a "scientific" reason for rejecting Christianity. According to this argument, there was not a shred of scientific justification for belief in God; and a man of intellectual integrity will not believe theories that lack scientific support; therefore a man of intellectual integrity will not believe in God. At the same time agnosticism conceded that there is no scientific proof that God does *not* exist. Nor is there any proof that Aphrodite and Apollo don't exist, or that elves and fairies don't exist. Thus the scientifically-minded agnostic, while leaving open the abstract—the exceedingly abstract—possibility that God (not to mention Aphrodite, Apollo, elves, and fairies) might exist, will in practice assume that God does not exist. And of course if a reasonable man cannot believe in the existence of God, then neither can he believe in the truth of Christianity. If you believe in Christianity, this, agnostics held, is a mark of both your scientific ignorance and your wishful thinking.

(2) Another agnostic argument against Christianity—and this was the single most popular argument—was derived from the revolution in biology that commenced in 1859 with the publication of Darwin's *The Origin of Species*. If Darwin's theory of evolution is true, or even approximately true, then the account of six days of creation given in the Book of Genesis is wildly erroneous; and thus, since Darwin's theory is true, the Bible is not literally true. And if the Bible is not true in the first chapters of its first book, then it is likely to be untrue in many other places as well. And if it is often, or even sometimes, untrue, then how can it be a work written, as Christians believe, by the Holy Spirit? But suppose a Christian were to drop his insistence that the Genesis account of creation is literally correct; suppose instead he were to say, as many Christians did, that the Genesis account is a poetic and symbolic myth. What then? Could the Darwinian theory still be used against his Christian belief? Yes, replied agnosticism. For evolution by means of random mutation and natural selection showed that the entire world of living things could be explained without any appeal to God. Everything was natural, nothing miraculous or supernatural. When it comes to the world of living things, God is an unneeded hypothesis. And although Darwin's theory of evolution was a purely biological theory, a theory limited to the evolution of living things, Darwin's success

in this biological realm of being makes it likely that a pre-biological cosmic evolution proceeded, and is still proceeding, in a similar way, that is, as a result of purely natural, non-miraculous causes.[55]

(3) Yet another agnostic argument against Christianity was borrowed from modern Biblical scholarship, more particularly the "higher criticism" scholarship whose principal home during the 19th century was Germany. German scholarship had done a great amount of "reverse engineering" of the Bible. That is, it had figured out—or at least tried to figure out—how the Bible had been constructed. This led to the rejection of many of the traditional authorships of Biblical books. For instance, the scholars agreed that Moses was not the author of the "five books of Moses," that King David was not the author of the Book of Psalms, that King Solomon was not the author of Proverbs or Ecclesiastes, and that the Book of Isaiah was made up of three parts written by three different authors at three different times. With regard to the New Testament, doubts were raised about authorship of the three Synoptic Gospels; there was something not far from a consensus that the Apostle John was not the author of the Fourth Gospel; and a number of letters traditionally attributed to St. Paul, it was agreed, had in fact not been written by him. The higher critics held that the present forms of many books of the Bible were the result, not of some single author, but of editors who had synthesized a variety of sources to produce a single work. Worse still from a traditional Christian point of view, the content of many books of the Bible, including the four New Testament Gospels, was a mélange of historical fact, of misremembered historical fact, of deliberately distorted historical fact, and of downright myth.

For the most part the German scholars had not intended that their Biblical criticism should serve to undermine the validity of Christianity; rather they hoped (as had the early Boston Unitarians) that their studies would lead to a modernized and purified Christianity. But it was easy enough for the agnostic movement—especially in Protestant countries, where according to the old

---

[55]   Herbert Spencer's theory of evolution, which antedated Darwin's theory, was a theory not so much of biological as of *cosmic* evolution. The success and prestige of Darwin's theory gave greatly added plausibility to Spencer's theory.

saying "the Bible is the religion of Protestantism"—to seize upon the higher criticism and use it to delegitimize Christianity. "Not only is there no evidence that God exists," said agnosticism, "but there is now abundant evidence that the holy book of Christianity, far from being a God-made thing, is a purely man-made thing; and that, moreover, the men who made it have often been deficient not only in scientific and historical knowledge but in simple honesty."

Two of the most striking characteristics of American agnosticism of this period were these. First, it was purely negative. It tried to destroy Christianity, but it had nothing positive to put in its place. Agnostics of the day seem to have believed that once Christianity was destroyed, it would be spontaneously replaced by a natural human love of goodness and truth. Liberated from the incubus of religion, the human race would immediately know how to use its new freedom in a happy way. Second, as noted above, although it claimed to occupy a skeptical middle ground between religious belief on the one hand and outright atheism on the other, in practice agnosticism was virtually indistinguishable from atheism. When pressed, the agnostic would allow that there was *some* possibility—an exceedingly slim one—that God might exist (or that the human soul might survive death). But in practice, the possibility that God exists was so slim that it did not have to be taken into consideration either when thinking or when acting. For all practical purposes, agnosticism was equivalent to atheism—as it still is today.

In the United States the best-known agnostic in the late 1800s was Robert Ingersoll (1833-99). A magnificent and captivating public speaker in an age in which grandiloquent oratory had not yet passed from the American scene, Ingersoll was an intellectual lightweight, and his attacks on religion in general and Christianity in particular were little more than warmed-over critiques and jokes that he could have found (and probably did find) in Voltaire and Tom Paine. Ingersoll is forgotten today, but a more famous agnostic, who flourished in the first third of the 20th century, is still remembered. I refer to the great lawyer, Clarence Darrow[56] (1857-1938), whose mightiest blow

---

[56] To catch the flavor of Darrow's agnosticism and anti-Christianity, see his entertaining if somewhat superficial autobiography, *The Story of My Life* (originally published by Scribner's in 1932; republished in 1996 by Da Capo Press).

against Christianity was not struck until very late in the day, well after the peak of purely negative agnosticism. The blow was struck in 1925 at Dayton, Tennessee, at the celebrated "Monkey Trial." Darrow was the lawyer for the defendant, John Scopes, who had deliberately, as a way of testing the law, violated the Tennessee statute banning the teaching of evolution in public schools. Darrow lost in the Tennessee courtroom, but he won in the larger court of American public opinion, making Fundamentalist Protestantism—which rejected without equivocation agnosticism, German higher criticism, and Darwinism—look ridiculous in the eyes of cultured and semi-cultured persons.[57]

If agnosticism was a purely negative attack on Christianity in the intellectual realm, Anarchism was a purely negative attack in the realm of practice. Anarchism was dedicated to the utter revolutionary destruction of what it saw as three great evil institutions—church, state, and capitalism. As for a plan of reconstruction of society on the morning after the revolution, Anarchism had no answer, and argued that no answer was needed. Human nature, free at long last from its ancient repression, would soon figure out what to do. Just erase the old evil institutions, and people will more or less spontaneously create new and better institutions—institutions based on democratic free co-operation.[58]

In response to the agnostic assault on Christianity, liberal Protestantism did what it always does: it created a via media between Christianity and its critics. Above I said that there were three agnostic arguments against Christianity: an epistemological argument, an argument from Darwinism, and an argument from German Biblical criticism. The typical liberal Protestant response was this. (1) If there is no rational or scientific basis for religious faith, let faith be based on feeling, especially ethical feeling. (2) Let us accept evolution, both biological and cosmic, but at the same time let us say that God, is the ultimate

---

[57] A very good account of the Scopes trial is given in the book, *Summer for the Gods*, by Edward J. Larson; published by Basic Books in 1997. The book was awarded the Pulitzer Prize in History.

[58] The two best-known American anarchists of the day were both natives of Russia, Emma Goldman (1869-1940) and her good friend Alexander Berkman (1870-1936).

source of evolution. (3) Let us retain the Bible as the fundamental basis of our religion and as inspired (in some very vague sense of that word) by God, while at the same time frankly admitting that the Bible is shot through with historical and scientific inaccuracies and with less-than-adequate moral ideals.

This halfway accommodation to agnosticism by the liberal religion of the late 19th and early 20th centuries led to a great liberal-versus-conservative split in the world of American Protestantism—the split between modernists and fundamentalists. Fundamentalists[59] regarded modernists as traitors to Christianity: they were not really Christians at all; their religion was a new religion,[60] a non-Christianity masquerading in Christian clothing, and rather skimpy clothing at that. From the modernist point of view, fundamentalism was folly, an attempt by ignorant non-intellectuals and anti-intellectuals to prevent Christianity from making the adjustments needed to render it plausible in a scientifically enlightened modern world.

Fourth Stage: Constructive Secularism

I have said that the third stage of American anti-Christianity, agnosticism, was an essentially negative thing. It wanted to get rid of Christianity, but it spent almost no time or effort planning for a positive replacement. It assumed that a happy replacement would pop up spontaneously. By contrast, anti-Christians of the fourth stage recognized that a replacement for religion in general and Christianity in particular would have to be found. They devoted little or no attention to the work of demolishing Christianity. That work, they

---

[59]   The names "fundamentalism" and "fundamentalists" derive from a series of dozens of articles written from an anti-modernist Protestant point of view. The writings first appeared beginning in 1909. In 1917 they were assembled and published in four volumes by the Biblical Institute of Los Angeles under the title of *The Fundamentals*. These four volumes were republished in 1998 by Baker Books.

[60]   For a good example of the argument that Protestant liberalism is a new religion, something other than Christianity, see the book by J. Gresham Machen, one of the most learned conservatives, *Christianity and Liberalism* (first published in 1923).

believed, had already been done. If Christianity still lingered in the world, it was the way a terminally ill person will often linger. The fatal blow had already been struck; it was now time to move on to the post-Christian future. Fourth-stage anti-Christianity concentrated on the construction of that future. The time span occupied by this fourth stage was, roughly, from early in the 20th century through the 1950s—which means that it overlapped in time with the third stage. (The first 15 or 20 years of the century were a period in which both third and fourth stage flourished.)

The most distinguished of these constructive secularists (as they may be called) was the philosopher John Dewey (1858-1952). Dewey in his long career was a professor at a number of leading universities (Michigan, Chicago, and Columbia), but more importantly he was a prolific writer on a wide variety of philosophical and non-philosophical subjects. He wrote on logic, metaphysics, ethics, aesthetics, psychology, politics, sociology, and—most notable of all—education; for it was through the schools, above all public schools, that the minds of younger generations would be prepared for living in a post-Christian world. Curiously, this atheist (who had been a Christian believer in his youth) also wrote on religion. In a book written late in his career, *A Common Faith* (1934), he proposed a new religion, a religion without God.[61] He even went so far in this book as to suggest that the word "God" be retained: but instead of denoting an actually existing being, it would now denote our highest ideals; and thus an atheistic person, provided he or she was sufficiently idealistic (like Dewey himself), could be said to believe in God. Needless to say, Dewey's notions of "God" and a godless religion never caught on; they seemed equally absurd to both Christians and secularists.

Dewey, like the agnostics of the third stage, was a great believer in the power of science to save us. Unlike third-stage agnostics, however, he was not so much interested in the *results* of science as in the *method*. To be sure, third-stage agnostics had been interested in scientific method too, but they were

---

[61] In making his proposal for an atheistic religion, Dewey was very probably influenced by the earlier idea of a "Religion of Humanity" put forwards by the French philosopher-sociologist Auguste Comte (1798-1857).

mostly interested in it as a stick with which to beat religion and Christianity. The scientific mind, they held, believes only that which can be demonstrated by evidence of the senses; and since Christianity cannot be scientifically demonstrated, the scientific mind will not accept it. Theirs, however, was a crude notion of scientific method; Dewey, by contrast, had a far more complex notion. Again and again he analyzed the workings of scientific thinking with a view to extending this mode of thinking to questions of morality and of social order and progress. He was not interested in using scientific thinking as a weapon to defeat Christianity. In his view, it had already been defeated. Hardly ever, except between the lines, does one find a criticism of Christianity in Dewey. In his time, because of the non-explicitness of his critique of Christianity, many Christians, especially those who were professional public school educators, read Dewey with approval, apparently not suspecting that he was a deadly enemy of their religion.

Felix Adler (1851-1933)—another Columbia University professor, where he was for many years a colleague of Dewey in the Philosophy Department—was a German Jew who migrated with his family to the United States in the early years of his life. His father was a rabbi, and when Felix was a young man he too intended to become a rabbi. He went back to Germany to study philosophy, and while there he underwent two notable mental/moral transformations, one negative, the other positive. Negatively, he lost his religious faith: he came to feel that it was impossible for a person with a modern mind to believe in God. Positively, he came under the influence of the moral philosophy of Immanuel Kant (1722-1804); Kantianism was undergoing a revival in Germany at the time. Regardless of whether or not God existed, Kant held, one had to obey the stern voice of moral duty. Back in the United States, Adler founded the Ethical Culture Society, which was dedicated to the proposition that a pure and demanding morality could exist quite independently of any theistic support. However, it could not exist independently of social support; hence the need to gather persons who were ethical but non-religious into a social group, a kind of secular "church"— which he called the Ethical Culture Society. Adler's *principal* focus was personal morality, not social reform; in this he differed from Dewey. But

Adler *was* interested in social reform; and this for two reasons. First, making society better was an ethical duty; and second, an improved society would make it easier for more people to be ethically good. In the gallery of American anti-Christians, Adler is one of the figures that Christians are most likely to find attractive. Yet his Ethical Culture Society, alas, never really caught on; it never spread much beyond Manhattan, where it survives today on the Upper West Side in a building facing Central Park and in a distinguished (and expensive) private school. In this regard it is reminiscent of Unitarianism, which never spread much beyond Boston. If Unitarianism is a tiny thing today, the Ethical Culture movement is tinier still; and apart from their names,[62] the two are now virtually indistinguishable from one another.

Dewey and Adler were university professors, temperate men who were out to reform the world gradually by means of education and rational persuasion, not to provoke it to violent revolution. But during this era of constructive secularism, would-be violent revolutionaries were not lacking in America, just as they were certainly not lacking in Europe and Asia at the same time. There was the Communist Party of the United States, which flourished from the 1920s till the 1950s, usually as a near-traitorous or fully traitorous instrument of the Soviet Union. Unlike Anarchism, which was purely negative, Communism was positive or constructive in that it held that the work of revolution would not be complete once the old order had been destroyed; no, a new order would have to be constructed. That's why the revolution would not proceed, as the Anarchists wished, to the immediate abolition of the state; instead it would transform the (bad) capitalist state into a (good) proletarian state; only later would the state gradually "wither away" (a phrase coined by Engels and endorsed by Lenin). American Communism drew a number of influential persons to it (Alger Hiss, for example, and many Hollywood people, and many young Jewish intellectuals in New York City). Although it was virulently anti-Christianity, it ended up—ironically and quite unintentionally—having more of a positive

---

[62]   In 1961 the Unitarians merged with the Universalists, so that today the official Unitarian name is the Unitarian Universalist Association.

than a negative impact on Christianity in America. Its association with the Soviet Union, the great enemy of the United States in the post-World War II period, made atheism, which was part and parcel of Communist doctrine, seem to be a decidedly un-American thing. It was routine in those days to refer to Communism as "godless Communism," the implication being that to be a good patriot one had to be a "God-fearing" American. The religious revival that swept the United States in the 1950s was due in no small part to a strong American aversion to Communism and all its pomps and works, including its atheism.

Generically similar to Communism in its wish to transform American society and its economy was Communism's less radical, but more popular, cousin, the American Socialist movement, which featured such luminaries as Eugene Debs and Norman Thomas. Socialists too wished to bring about an American revolution, but not a violent one: instead a gradual revolution achieved through rational persuasion of the electorate. Socialists were in the order of practice what Dewey was in the order of theory. Anti-Christianity, an essential ingredient of Communism, was *not* an essential ingredient of American Socialism; and more than a few liberal Protestant clerics were supporters of Socialism. Indeed the six-time Socialist Party candidate for president, Norman Thomas, had early in his career been ordained as a Protestant minister. But it is safe to say that most pro-Socialism Americans had scant sympathy for Christianity, or rather no sympathy at all. They were secularists, but of the quiet kind. They did not shout, "Down with Christianity." They shouted only, "Up with Socialism." Like Dewey and Adler, they felt sure that Christianity and all other possible forms of supernaturalistic religion had had their day and were now dead, though perhaps not yet buried. The task in front of us, they felt, was to reconstruct civilization on a godless basis.

If I am correct when I say (as I have been saying again and again in this book) that liberal Christianity always tries to blend—quite incoherently—Christianity with the fashionable anti-Christianity of its day, then we should expect to find during the era I am currently speaking of a blend of Christianity with radical social reconstruction, whether the highly intellectualized reconstructionism of intellectuals like Dewey or the activist reconstructionism of the Communists and their more moderate cousins, the Socialists. And so we do find this blend—in the Social Gospel movement.[63] This movement was an attempt to blend Christian thought and morality with the concerns of certain anti-Christian political movements—Socialism and Communism. These anti-Christianity movements were concerned with the misery of the lower classes, above all the urban working classes. The Social Gospel movement in the United States (like the Christian Socialist movement in England) had a twofold aim: (1) to meliorate the condition of the working classes, and (2) to keep the working classes within the Christian fold, preventing them from being seduced and captured by anti-Christian parties. In the process of doing this, liberal Christianity once again did what it always does: it created an amalgam made up of elements of Christianity (love of neighbor in this case) with elements of anti-Christianity (in this case Socialistic ideals and practical proposals).

When I point this out, I am not necessarily finding fault with the Social Gospel movement; for I personally think the Social Gospel is one of the noblest achievements in the long history of American Protestantism. But the danger here was a danger that often appears when Christianity is combined with its opposite, namely, that the opposite element eventually gets the upper hand. This happened, at least to a very notable extent, to the Social Gospel movement. In time the religious element grew weaker, increasingly becoming little more than rhetoric, while the practical proposals for social reform—Socialist-inspired proposals that almost always required governmental action—grew increasingly predominant. There seems to be something like a sociological law at work here: whenever you blend Christianity with some kind of anti-Christianity, the anti-Christian element will sooner or later get the upper hand.

---

[63]   The landmark book, which may be said to mark the beginning (though perhaps not the *very* beginning) of the Social Gospel movement was *Christianity and the Social Crisis* by Walter Rauschenbusch, first published in 1907.

Fifth Stage: the Sexual Revolution

Earlier in the book I spoke of a different kind of attack on Christianity, an attack that was purely practical and not at all theoretical—the "sexual revolution" (SR) that came to full flower in the 1960s and '70s. Virtually overnight, sexual conduct that for many centuries had been condemned by Christianity as sinful became in the opinion of great numbers of Americans, especially those of the younger generation, perfectly acceptable. Premarital sex became morally allowable not only in the eyes of the young but in the eyes of many sympathetic elders. Even casual premarital sex became allowable; it was no longer necessary for unmarried sexual partners to be "in love" with one another before jumping into bed together. Unmarried cohabitation became allowable; and in more recent decades "living together" has come to be seen by many young Americans—perhaps even most—as something like a prerequisite for marriage. ("You wouldn't buy a car without test-driving it first, would you?") It became allowable for unmarried women/girls to bear children. And it also became allowable for the fathers of these out-of-wedlock children to take little or no responsibility for their offspring; the old pre-SR rule, that if you got a girl pregnant you had to marry her, was quietly abolished. Abortion too came to be seen as morally allowable—for how can we have a regime of sexual permissiveness if we don't have abortion as an ace-in-the-hole to correct "mistakes"? The moral permission to have and to provide abortions became a *legal* permission in January of 1973 when the United States Supreme Court issued its notorious *Roe v. Wade* ruling, and this ruling in turn strongly reinforced the belief that abortion is morally acceptable. For the traditional American belief has always been that the rights protected by the Constitution are God-given rights; and so if the Constitution protects a right to abortion, then the right to abortion must be something very similar to a God-given right— or at least a fundamental moral right. Getting divorced became far easier as public opinion grew more tolerant of divorce, as the social stigma on divorced persons was lifted, and as state after state enacted "no-fault" divorce laws. Again, this followed quite logically from the idea of sexual freedom; for how could a person be sexually free if he or she had to remain chained to a marital partner chosen years earlier? Of spouses married years earlier, one spouse may have "grown" and the other not; or they may both have "grown," but in two different directions. Tolerance of homosexuality developed more slowly than tolerance of other kinds of traditionally prohibited sexual conduct, but it did develop. And if today, almost a half-century after the beginning of the SR, we have more than a few states in which same-sex marriage is legally permitted, this is one of the late-blooming flowers of the SR of the '60s and '70s.

All this was a massive, and for the most part very sudden, repudiation of the traditional sexual ethic that had been common to both Catholics and Protestants. And since the sexual ethic of Christianity has never been a merely incidental feature of the religion, but a central and essential element, it may be said that whoever repudiates the sexual ethic of Christianity repudiates Christianity itself. The SR, then, was a de facto attack on Christianity; it was in its day the latest form of anti-Christianity, the latest form of secularism.

Note that when I speak of the SR I am not speaking of the mere fact that people were *behaving* in ways that Christianity had always condemned as sinful. That many people would commit sexual sins was nothing new in the world. What was new was the fact that they would commit these sins while at the same time *denying that they were sinful*. In the old pre-SR era, people committed these sins without pretending that they were something other than sins. They said, "This is naughty, but I rather enjoy it; so I'll do it anyway." In the new era these "sins" were declared to be perfectly sinless. More, they were often considered to be virtuous: an important part of the maturation process; a way of building character.

Although the sexual revolution came to fruition in the '60s and '70s, the seeds had been planted far earlier. Margaret Sanger (1879-1966), the "mother of birth control" in America, was perhaps the first notable champion of the revolution. What she promoted, the ready availability of contraceptives for married couples, seems pretty tame today when compared with other and later kinds of sexual liberty; but she opened the door for what was to come. In demanding a right to contraception, however, she was demanding more than a narrow particular right; she was demanding a broad general principle, namely the right to separate sex from reproduction. Once that principle was established, it was only a matter of time before logical conclusions would be drawn. If sex and reproduction can be divorced from one another in marriage, then why not outside of marriage? If premarital sex could be engaged in without risk of pregnancy, then much of the practical—and even moral—objection to premarital sex, whether in a casual situation or in the context of unmarried cohabitation, vanished. Further, if sex could be divorced from reproduction, didn't it follow that homosexuality is tolerable, since homosexual conduct has *always* divorced sex from reproduction? As for abortion—well, that would be necessary to clean up any "mistakes" that happened under the new regime. The nice upper and upper-middle class Protestant ladies who assisted Sanger in her birth control crusade[64] may not have foreseen all this, and almost certainly most of them would have disapproved of it if they *had* foreseen it; yet the entire sexual revolution was implicit—present in germ, so to speak—in Sanger's struggle for marital contraception.

Sanger, by the way, clearly understood that her plea for contraception was an argument against traditional Christianity, above all against Catholicism; for it was Catholic bishops and priests who were her principal foes. Whether they realized it or not at the time (some of them did, some of them didn't), it was not just birth control for married couples they were fighting against; they were fighting against the pending sexual revolution—trying to kill it when it was still in its embryonic state, as it were. In the end it was Sanger (ironically, she had been baptized Catholic as a child) who prevailed while you bishops and your priests went down to ignominious defeat. You went down to defeat even among your own people; for the great majority of American Catholics today disagree with the Church's teaching on contraception. When it comes to contraception, Catholics today are Sangerites far more than they are papists.

The heyday of Margaret Sanger was in the decades between the two world wars. During that era and for another 20 years after World War II, her great de facto ally in the pilgrimage toward sexual liberation was Sigmund Freud; or rather, it was those of Freud's American fans who, thanks to a vulgar

---

[64]   One of the most notable of these assistants, operating mainly in her home state of Connecticut, was the mother of the famous movie actress Katherine Hepburn.

misunderstanding of his teachings, took Freud to be an advocate of radical sexual liberation. Now while Freud was an opponent of the hyper-repression that often characterized Victorian sexual attitudes, especially the sexual attitudes of girls and women, he was certainly not the enemy of sexual repression generally. He believed (as can be seen most clearly in his small book *Civilization and Its Discontents*) that sexual repression, and a fairly serious degree of sexual repression at that, was necessary for the advance of civilization. He favored *some* sexual liberation, but only a modest amount. Yet that's not the way many of his American followers understood him; they saw him as the great prophet of radical sexual liberation. It is interesting to note that Freud's reputation, which stood high in America for nearly half a century (from the end of World War I till about 1965), suddenly collapsed at about the time the SR triumphed in the United States. If his popularity rested to a great extent on his image as a prophet of sexual liberation in the days when there was no such thing, what need would there be for him once the real thing arrived?[65]

In addition to Sanger and Freud there was Albert Kinsey (1894-1956), the sex researcher from the University of Indiana, who along with a number of associates produced two culture-shaking books in the years just following World War II, *Sexual Behavior in the Human Male* (published in 1948) and *Sexual Behavior in the Human Female* (1953).[66] It is not probable that many people actually read and digested Kinsey's ponderous and statistics-laden tomes, but millions became acquainted with the findings reported in these volumes, at least the more sensational among these findings, by means of second-hand and

---

[65] It should be acknowledged that there were at least two other causes for the collapse of his fame, feminism and the gay movement. Feminists didn't like him because of his theory of "penis envy," and gays didn't like him because of his theory that homosexuality is the result of psychosexual immaturity.

[66] The titles of the books were misleading, since it was not timeless and universal "human" sexual behavior that Kinsey studied, but the sexual behavior of 20th century American males and females. You can study universal human anatomy and physiology, but you cannot study universal human conduct since, man being a cultural animal, there is no such thing as universal human conduct. All conduct takes place within the context of, and is shaped by, this or that particular culture.

third-hand reports in newspapers and magazines. What Kinsey found[67] was that Americans engaged in what was conventionally regarded as illicit sex—in particular, premarital sex, adultery, and homosexuality—to a far greater extent than most people had hitherto believed. Moreover, the incidence of illicit sex was increasing as generations went by; and so, if in the late '40s and early '50s it was happening at a higher rate than in the early decades of the 20th century, it would very probably be happening at a much higher rate still in decades to come.

It is conceivable that there might have been a strongly traditionalist reaction to Kinsey's findings. Believers in the Christian ideal of chastity might have said: "Oh, this is dreadful. Let's make a strenuous effort to restore good sexual morality to America. Let's have a purity crusade." Some had this reaction, but not many. The typical reaction to Kinsey took two forms. The more puritanical form simply denied that his findings were accurate: "In general, we Americans are sexually pure; Kinsey has slandered us." On the other hand there were reactions that were more or less libertarian. Either: "I used to think that my sexual behavior was abnormal, and so I had a bad conscience about it; but I now see that it is not abnormal at all, so henceforth I'll have a good conscience." Or: "I see that my fellow-Americans are much more sexually liberated than I have been; so I'll have to catch up; in the future I will increase my degree of sexual liberation."

Thanks to Sanger and Freud and Kinsey, the ground had been intellectually prepared, and in the 1960s a generation of middle-class kids, who had been born after World War II and had grown up in suburban prosperity, revolutionized American sexual morality. What before had been taboo was now permitted, and often applauded, and in many cases virtually required.

As I stressed above, this was not simply a case of "immoral" sexual conduct. Rather it was a case of declaring that what our foolish parents and teachers and clergy had hitherto imagined to be immoral conduct was not immoral at all;

---

[67] Some of his critics have contended that Kinsey didn't really "find" what he thought he had found; for, according to the critics, the samples he studied were not truly representative samples of the American population.

what they thought sinful was in fact sinless; what they thought bad was in fact good. From a Catholic point of view, what was going on was not simply sexual sin; it was sexual *heresy* (to use an old-fashioned but accurate word). The sexual revolutionaries were saying that the sexual teachings of Catholic Church (and of other churches as well) had been erroneous for many centuries. And if the churches were in error on so obvious a thing as sexual morality, how many other things must they have got wrong too?

The Silence of the Shepherds

And what were you bishops doing while the sexual revolution of the 1960s and '70s was happening?[68] For the most part you were sitting on your hands and biting your tongues as Catholics began behaving and thinking like sexually liberated Americans—as Catholics of the younger generation began sleeping around, as adultery among Catholics increased in frequency, as no-fault divorce swept the land, as Catholic divorce rates sky-rocketed, as contraception became nearly universal among Catholic married couples of child-bearing age, as Catholics began having abortions like other Americans, and as Catholics increasingly muttered (and sometimes shouted from the rooftops): "When will my Church adopt a more modern and more reasonable sexual morality?" You bishops did stir, it is true, when in January of 1973 the United States Supreme Court handed down its appalling *Roe v. Wade* ruling, declaring the right to abortion to be a constitutionally guaranteed right. You denounced the Court decision, and your denunciations helped, at least for a while, to stimulate the prolife movement. But hitherto you had allowed the SR to proceed almost without protest; and since belief in a right to abortion is a logical consequence

---

[68]   I am of course well aware that hardly any, if any at all, of the bishops in office today were bishops during the 1960s and '70s; many were not even ordained as priests at that now-distant period. But as I said near the beginning of this book, when I speak of the deficiencies of the bishops I am speaking of the deficiencies of the episcopal *order*; and if you belong to that order, you share in the collective responsibility of that order.

of the SR, it is small wonder that a specific denunciation of abortion would not have much impact when it was not part of a more comprehensive denunciation of and resistance to the SR. And indeed the abortion denunciation did not have much impact among Catholics. A few Catholics became activists in the anti-abortion movement, but the great majority of Catholics either approved of abortion, or were willing to tolerate it, or disapproved of it in a not-very-strenuous way, or adopted a neutral attitude. A sign of this is the fact that states with the highest percentage of Catholics in their population have routinely sent, and continue to send, pro-abortion senators and representatives—many of them Catholic themselves—to Washington; think for example of the late Teddy Kennedy, a Catholic pro-abortion senator from Massachusetts, a state with a population nearly 50 percent Catholic. If the prolife movement is a formidable factor in American life today, as it certainly is, this is to the credit not so much of Catholics and their bishops as of conservative Protestants.

Of course there is an excuse that can be offered for the inaction of bishops in response to the SR. "The 1960s," you bishops can say, "was the time of Vatican II, and after the council the Catholic Church in America looked for a while like it was coming apart at the seams. Sunday Mass attendance dropped suddenly and precipitously; thousands of priests abandoned the priesthood; tens of thousands of nuns fled the convent; it became nearly impossible to recruit new nuns and priests; Catholic schools closed left and right; Catholic colleges and universities began de-Catholicizing themselves; and so on. We bishops had enough in-house problems to worry about without worrying about the American sexual revolution as well." In rebuttal to this, it can be contended with some plausibility that if the bishops had strenuously resisted the SR, the in-house erosion and collapse would not have been as extensive as it turned out to be. Waiving that point, however, I will simply remind you of the old Harry Truman maxim, quoted earlier: "The buck stops here." If you fail as leaders of the Catholic community, you have to take the blame, regardless of mitigating circumstances. Mitigating circumstances might exculpate you for not getting an A-plus or even a B-plus. But they don't exculpate you when you get a grade of F, and it was a grade of F that bishops deserved during the era of the SR.

Even worse: liberal Protestantism and the sexual revolution

But things might have been even worse. Take a look, for example, at the liberal Protestant response to the SR. Protestant liberalism (or liberal Protestantism if one prefers phrasing it that way), as I have contended above, has the centuries-old habit of trying to find a via media between traditional Christianity and the fashionable secularism of the day. Well, the fashionable secularism that began in the 1960s was a moral secularism that endorsed and promoted sexual liberation. And so, faithful to its nature, liberal Protestantism gave a kind of halfway or three-quarters endorsement of sexual liberation while cloaking this endorsement in the vocabulary of Christianity. "God is still speaking to us" has recently been the mantra of the United Church of Christ, the most decidedly liberal of all Protestant denominations,[69] but it could well be the slogan of all liberal/modernist Protestants—and "God is still speaking to us" means, when translated into plain English, that God has changed his/her ever-loving mind on matters related to sex. And what precisely does God tell us about sex when he/she speaks today? Well, he/she tells us, of course, that the old Christian rules against fornication and unmarried cohabitation don't hold anymore. And he/she also tells us, with regard to homosexuality, that we should disregard thousands of years of Jewish-Christian tradition (including Paul's strictures in the first chapter of his Epistle to the Romans); instead we should endorse homosexual conduct, at least in many circumstances. God tells us that he/she has given some people a homosexual nature from birth, and wishes those persons to engage in homosexual relations with partners of a like nature. God even tells us to ordain openly gay and lesbian ministers and bishops. Of course God doesn't go so far as to endorse homosexual hedonistic promiscuity. God does not say, according to liberal Protestantism, "You gays should pick up a different guy in a gay bar almost every night. In your youth, while you still have your looks and your stamina, you should have scores of sexual partners

---

[69]   Ironically, one of the constituent sub-denominations of the UCC is the Congregational Church, the church of the great 18th century Calvinist theologian Jonathan Edwards. Poor Edwards! He must be spinning in his grave to think what his church has become.

each year." No, he/she prefers that two gays or two lesbians have a "loving" relationship—although God, being a God of love and forgiveness (in other words, being a morally liberal God), doesn't get especially upset if a certain amount of immature promiscuous experimentation precedes the discovery of this loving and stable mature relationship. The best-known instance of Christian endorsement of homosexuality was found in the Episcopal Church, which in 2003 approved of the ordination of an openly gay bishop in New Hampshire, Bishop Gene Robinson, and in the summer of 2009 gave general approval to the ordination, both to the priesthood and to the episcopacy, of sexually active homosexuals.[70] In general, liberal Protestantism has found, and still is finding, ways to endorse the agenda of the SR—pre-marital sex, cohabitation, abortion, homosexuality, etc. But these endorsements are given in a "Christian" way; that is, they are accompanied by admonitions that these hitherto illicit sexual relationships must be conducted in such a way that the partners respect the humanity and the children-of-God-ness of one another. The via media raises its watered-down Christianity head once again. And by now the Christianity of present-day liberal Protestantism is very watered-down indeed.

To anyone who is in the slightest degree familiar with what Christianity has been in the course of its long history, the belief that religious liberals of today hold, namely that their endorsement of sexual freedom can count as a kind of Christianity, is not only an absurdity; it is an astonishing act of self-deception. You Catholic bishops, deficient as you have been in many ways, are at least not as deficient in your idea of Christianity as liberal Protestants have been. In fact you are far, far from it. So I congratulate you for that at least. At the same time, you have millions of laypersons, and probably thousands of priests and nuns, who are full of the same self-deception that characterizes liberal Protestants. You bishops have done relatively little to fight against this toxic liberalism. Alas.

[end of chapter]

---

[70] The approval of the Robinson ordination has led to serious ruptures in the Episcopal Church and in the larger worldwide Anglican Communion, as traditionalists have fought back against liberal modernists. The 2009 action has led to still further ruptures.

CHAPTER 6

The Sixth Stage

During the years 2006 and 2007 there was a curious development on best-seller lists, a development that suggests that the United States has entered a new and more intensified stage of the "culture war" between Christianity and secularism. The first five stages of American secularism were outlined in the preceding chapter. In this chapter I will discuss the latest or sixth stage of American secularism.

The evidence I have in mind when I speak of the sixth stage of American secularism are five[71] very popular books—pro-atheism writings that have made it to the best-seller lists and very openly assail theism in general and Christianity in particular:

- *The God Delusion*, by Richard Dawkins
- *God is Not Great*, by Christopher Hitchens
- *Breaking the Spell*, by Daniel Dennett;

---

[71] There have been other anti-Christianity books that have sold well in recent years, but the five I list have been the most conspicuous.

- *The End of Faith,* by Sam Harris
- *Letter to a Christian Nation,* [72] also by Harris

A sociologically interesting thing about these anti-Christian, pro-atheism best-sellers is that they violate what had been, beginning early in the 20th century, an unwritten rule of American cultural good manners, namely, that you are not supposed to attack the religious beliefs of a fellow American in a public way. This rule meant that Protestants were expected to abandon their old practice of denouncing Catholicism as a perverted version of Christianity, and Catholics were supposed to abstain from denouncing Protestantism as a severely truncated version of true Christianity. Of course you could say these things if you really wanted to—provided you said them privately, either at home or inside the walls of your own churches or schools; but you mustn't shout them from the rooftops, or broadcast them over radio or television, or write them in books published by respectable publishing houses. And if Catholics and Protestants had to show a tender respect for one another's religious feelings, they both had to respect the religious feelings of Jews: public denunciation of Jews and Judaism became strictly prohibited, especially after World War II and the Holocaust.

It followed from this that atheists and agnostics were not allowed to attack theism in general or Christianity in particular. There was of course no *law* against such attacks except for the "law" of good manners. For an unbeliever to attack Christianity was regarded as a great breach of courtesy. The only well-known atheist who was guilty of this breech on a regular basis was an Englishman, the famous mathematician-philosopher Bertrand Russell, whose books (including *Why I Am not a Christian*) always sold well in the United States. It is as if American atheists and agnostics, finding hardly any native writer who would give voice to their covert disdain for Christianity, had to import a foreign author.

---

[72]   This last book is so brief—less than 100 pages of text, and not many words per page—that it hardly deserves to be called a "book." "Pamphlet" would be a more correct name. All the same, it made it to the best-seller lists and remained there a long time.

This rule—that religious believers had to respect (or at least pretend to respect) the religious beliefs of those who held a different religion, and that non-believers had to respect (or pretend to respect) all religious beliefs—may have been of dubious intellectual or philosophical value; but it clearly had great social value. It is easier for members of a religiously diverse society to get along with one another if they abstain from inter-religious criticism.

One notable and rather inconsistent feature of this taboo was that it did not require reciprocity between theists and atheists. Atheists were expected to abstain from criticizing religion, yet religious believers were *not* expected to abstain from criticizing atheism. The reason for this was that Americans saw themselves as an essentially religious nation in which atheists were nothing more than a small, deviant, and unimportant minority. It didn't matter which particular religion you belonged to, but as a good American you should adhere to *some* religion. During the first decade or so of the Cold War, it was the most normal thing in the world for those defending the American way of life to denounce Communism as being "atheistic" or "godless." The clear implication here was that atheism is a very bad thing. And if Communism, a bad thing to begin with, was made even worse by being atheistic, then non-Communist American atheists, while not as bad as their "red" fellow unbelievers, must be pretty bad. Another way of putting this is to say that during the middle years of the 20th century atheists were excluded from the theistic consensus—the Judeo-Christian consensus—that dominated American cultural life. Just as African-Americans were "second-class citizens" by virtue of belonging to the "wrong" race, so atheists were second-class by virtue of having wrong views on religion.

Those days are gone—and probably gone forever, despite the wishes of some cultural conservatives who would like once again to define the United States as a Christian or Judeo-Christian nation. Though still relatively small in number, atheists are disproportionately represented, as noted earlier, in what may be called the "command posts" of American culture—I refer to elite universities (including law schools), the mainstream media, and the entertainment industry. Their influence in American economic life and political life (most notably in the Democratic Party) is very great. It is unlikely that theistic Americans will ever again be able to forget that many of their fellow-Americans are atheists, or to pretend that this atheistic minority simply doesn't count.[73]

Just as the Supreme Court's *Brown* decision of 1954 gave a signal to the nation that the days of second-class citizenship for blacks were bound to come to an end, so, although rather less dramatically, the Court's school prayer ruling of 1962 (*Engel v. Vitale*) signaled that the second-class status of atheists was bound to come to an end. Under our theistic or Judeo-Christian consensus, it was understood that schools should not compel students to say prayers that might be offensive to members of this or that religious denomination; and so any mandatory school prayer would have to be nonsectarian or non-denominational.[74] The Court's 1962 ruling in effect extended this "sensitivity test" (as it may be called) to atheists. Just as there must be no Christian prayers that offend Jews and no Protestant prayers that offend Catholics, so there must be no prayers that offend atheists. But *all* prayers offend atheists; therefore there must be no prayers at all.

It is more than half a century since that famous decision, and in the interval the atheistic element in American society has grown in numbers and in power. Up till recently this atheism manifested itself mostly in practical conduct, not in theoretical manifestos. Atheists continued for the most part to observe the good-manners rule that you mustn't criticize the other fellow's religion; yet increasing numbers of people deliberately lived their lives as if God does not exist; more specifically, they lived their lives as though God as conceived by Christianity does not exist. They were, we may say, "practical atheists" if not always theoretical atheists. As noted in the immediately preceding chapter, the sexual revolution of the 1960s and '70s—giving as it did its stamp of approval to a wide-range of decidedly un-Christian behaviors: pornography, premarital sex

---

[73] In the present discussion I am counting almost all "agnostics" as atheists, since the great majority of American agnostics are virtual atheists for all practical purposes.

[74] The prayer said in most schools was The Lord's Prayer (Our Father). This, a prayer from the New Testament, was mutually acceptable to Protestants and Catholics; and although its provenance was objectionable from a Jewish point of view, its content was not.

(fornication), unmarried cohabitation, no-fault divorce, abortion, homosexuality, etc.—has been the most striking instance of this practical atheism.

Although it may be too early to be certain (time will tell), my guess is that the atheistic best-sellers I mentioned at the beginning of this chapter mark a new stage in the history of American secularism or anti-Christianity. The atheists of America are "coming out of the closet." They are passing from a stage of practical atheism (which is where they have been ever since the beginning of the sexual revolution) to a stage of practical-plus-theoretical atheism. That is to say, practical atheism will continue (in the form of sexual liberty, abortion, same-sex marriage, and perhaps euthanasia), but it will be supplemented by theoretical defenses of atheism and overt, articulate attacks upon Christianity.

A danger and an opportunity

If I am correct about this development, it presents both a danger and an opportunity to American Catholicism and to you Catholic bishops. This overt atheism is obviously a danger, since it will permit pro-atheism propagandists to seduce not a few Catholics from the faith, especially young Catholics. Many of the current attacks on Christianity, it is true, are nothing but warmed-over versions of the criticisms made in the 18th century by the likes of Voltaire and Tom Paine and in the 19th century by "agnostics" who wielded anti-Christianity weapons manufactured out of a skeptical epistemology, the Darwinian theory of evolution, or the German higher criticism of the Bible. Philosophically or theologically sophisticated Catholics have long since concluded that these old attacks, while sometimes clever and often challenging, miss the mark and leave the faith essentially undamaged. But the typical young Catholic is not philosophically or theologically sophisticated; indeed the typical young Catholic nowadays is not even moderately well-informed about the contents of his/her religion. So the new out-of-the-closet atheism is likely to draw many young people away from Catholicism, especially when combined, as it usually is, with the practical atheism of the sexual revolution.

Yet the new atheism is an opportunity as well. The enemy is no longer hidden, he is now out in the open; and other things being equal, it is easier to fight a visible foe than a concealed one. One of the great deficiencies in American Catholic life since the 1960s is that the leadership of the Church in this country—I mean you bishops and your priests—seem for the most part not to have realized that a massive attack was being made on Christianity in the form of practical atheism. You seem to have felt that the sexual revolution was no more than a sexual revolution, and that abortion was no more than abortion, and that homosexuality was no more than homosexuality. You did not realize that these things were the spearheads of practical atheism; nor did you realize that a culture becoming friendly to sexual liberty and abortion and homosexual marriage is a culture becoming correspondingly unfriendly to Christianity. You leaders seem to have believed that you were still living in an older America, an America that was hospitable to Christianity in general and to Catholicism in particular, the America of the decades of the 1930s, 1940s, and 1950s. You were mistaken about this, badly mistaken. But the new atheism (as reflected in the best-sellers listed above) will probably prevent you from deluding yourselves any longer. Realizing the danger, you will now, one hopes, have no choice but to fight back.

Of course when I say "you" with reference to our Catholic bishops and priests, this is a misleading word. The older generation of priests and bishops, men who grew up under the old America-is-friendly-to-Christianity dispensation, is passing, or has already passed, from the scene. It is being replaced by a younger generation of Church leaders, men who from their childhood have lived in a culture strongly permeated with practical atheism and anti-Christianity. The fact that these men chose the clerical life in this hostile cultural climate suggests that their decision was not just a choice *for* the priesthood but a choice *against* secularism and atheism. You younger bishops, then, are far more likely than your elders to be sensitive to the danger, and the new theoretical atheism should only increase your sensitivity.

I said the Church will have to "fight back." But how? In the old days, when Catholics in the United States were mostly immigrants of European ancestry or the children of such immigrants, there was a need to protect them from being seduced by the dominant American religion, Protestantism. This was done by creating a Catholic "ghetto." An attempt was made to shield Catholics from the influence of Protestant ideas. Catholics were discouraged from marrying Protestants, from reading Protestant books (they were even forbidden to read Protestant translations of the Bible[75]), and from attending Protestant schools and colleges. They were even discouraged from sending their kids to public schools if a parochial or diocesan school alternative was available. A vast alternative system of Catholic schools and colleges was created. Catholics could not be kept from reading non-Catholic newspapers, but their secular reading was supplemented by a Catholic press that produced great numbers of newspapers, magazines, and books.

To a great degree the ghetto worked—at least it did so until the 1960s, when its "walls" fell down.[76] During the ghetto era Catholics were for the most part kept within the Catholic fold. It was only a rare Catholic who drifted into Protestantism. But can a solution along these lines work against the new atheism? Can a new Catholic ghetto be constructed, this time to shield Catholics not from Protestant ideas but from far more dangerous atheistic or secularist ideas? I think not. The clock of history does not run backwards. The old Catholic ghetto is like Humpty-Dumpty: once destroyed, you can't put it together again.

So what is to be done? Atheism (and by "atheism" here I mean both practical and theoretical atheism) will have to be confronted directly in the marketplace of competing ideas and values. Catholic intellectuals, both clerical and lay, will have to reply to the atheistic intellectuals who "prove" that theism and Christianity are wrong; and they will have to make these replies, not simply in Catholic forums, but in the larger forum of American intellectual life. Catholic education will have to be strengthened and expanded, so that ordinary Catholics will be equipped with the knowledge needed to withstand attacks on their faith. And when I say "Catholic education" I don't refer only

---

[75] Including that classic of English literature, the Authorized (or King James) Version.

[76] For an account of the ghetto and its collapse, see my book *The Decline and Fall of the Catholic Church in America* (Sophia Institute Press, 2003), chapters 2 and 3.

---

to Catholic schools and colleges, where children and young persons get their religious education. I mean that a strenuous effort will have to be made—through homilies, lectures, seminars, discussion groups, Bible study groups, periodicals, books, book clubs, etc.—to reach *adult* Catholics. In general, the specifically Catholic element in the intellectual life of American Catholics will have to be elevated far above where it is at the moment. Indeed it will have to be elevated far above where it has ever been.

And then there is the question of moral values. Catholics will have to see clearly that a Christian way of life—with its emphasis on such "strange" virtues as chastity and humility and piety—is radically different from the currently fashionable way of life, that is, the way of life of practical atheism. They will have to understand that it is impossible to do what many of today's Catholics[77] think can be done, namely, blend Christianity and practical atheism. Most important of all, there will be a need for American Catholicism to produce more than a few *saints*—that is, individual Catholics who conspicuously bear witness to the validity of their religion by openly living Christian lives in defiance of the moral norms prescribed by practical atheism.

Will it be an easy thing to do? Not at all. It will be the most difficult thing in the world. But the emergence of explicit theoretical atheism, the kind represented by the best-sellers I mentioned at the outset of this chapter, at least gives us—and especially it gives you, the bishops—a chance to begin. We should keep in mind what a great philosopher[78] once said: "But all things excellent are as difficult as they are rare."

[end of chapter]

---

[77]   I refer to Catholics with a theologically "liberal" point of view.

[78]   Spinoza: the final sentence of his *Ethics*.

CHAPTER 7

The Social-Political Basis of Anti-Christianity

Earlier in the book (Chapter Four) I described the philosophy—more accurately, the ideology[79]—of secularist anti-Christianity. But no ideology can flourish without a social base; some group or set of groups has to be the "carrier" or "bearer" of the ideology. What is the social base of present-day American secularism? Who are its carriers?

Secularism's Social Class Foundation

Its social base is mainly "upscale" or upper-middle class (UMC) in character. So let me first give a brief sketch of what I have in mind when I speak of UMC people.

- To begin with, they are well educated. Almost always they have college degrees, and their degrees often come from high-prestige state or private colleges (e.g., Ivy League or outstanding state universities).

---

[79] When I speak of an ideology I mean what may be called a "fighting philosophy," that is, a philosophy used as a weapon in a struggle for social and cultural dominance.

Almost as a matter of course they have advanced degrees as well: very commonly an MA or MS, and often an MBA, a Ph.D., a JD, or an MD.

- Normally they are married to, or will eventually marry, a spouse with a similarly high level of formal education.
- Having a high level of education, they correspondingly have a high level of income, for in the US there is a strong correlation between income and education levels.
- Having high incomes, they have, at least by the middle of their adult lives, quite a lot in the way of wealth or assets. At some point in their 40s or 50s most of them have become millionaires—at least if we take "millionaire" according to its old definition (net *assets* of more than one million dollars) and not according to what seems to be on the way to becoming its newer definition (net *income* of at least one million dollars per year).
- They own handsome and well-furnished houses or condos or apartments; they often own a second home that they use for vacations.
- They own two or three good automobiles (except when they live in a densely populated urban place like Manhattan's Upper West Side, in which case they may not own a car at all).
- With either their time or their money or both, they contribute generously to charities and to other "good causes."[80]
- They take more than a passing interest in current literature and the arts.
- They send their kids (of which they have only a small number) to good public schools; or if they happen to live in a community that lacks good public schools,[81] they send the kids to good private schools.

---

[80] For the secularist UMC person these good causes would of course include Planned Parenthood and the ACLU.

[81] Why would they bother to live in communities lacking good public schools? Because they often like to live in big cities that have such desirable things as good UMC jobs, good symphonies, good museums, good bookstores, good art galleries, good restaurants, etc. Big cities of this kind are, however, notorious for undesirable public schools filled with low-income minorities, and white UMC secularists, though very favorably disposed to minorities as a matter of principle (and very censorious regarding white persons of any class who are not favorably disposed to minorities), generally don't want their own kids going to public schools with minority kids.

- They take long-distance vacation trips once or twice per year; often these vacations are taken abroad.
- They appreciate and consume good wine, good food, and good coffee.
- Their household incomes are, let us say, between $200,000 and $1,000,000 per year.

Let me broaden my definition a bit by saying that the UMC I have in mind is made up not only of people who *actually* have the characteristics I just listed; it is also made up of those who have these characteristics *potentially*, that is, people who *realistically aspire* to those characteristics. Many a young man or woman who is in graduate school or professional school, for instance, while being for the moment poorer than many slum-dwellers, aspires to eventual UMC status—and this aspiration is quite realistic. Such aspirants think and feel in an upper-middle class way, not because they already have the acquirements that provide the material base for those thoughts and feelings, but because they anticipate having those acquirements one of these days; what's more, by thinking and feeling in a UMC way, they accelerate their ascent into that class. Some who ascend into that class were born and grew up in working or lower-middle class families. But many others were born and grew up with UMC parents: they "ascend" not in the sense that they come from elsewhere but in the sense that they have to re-achieve what their parents (and maybe grandparents) achieved before them.

I hasten to add that I don't mean to say that *all* UMC people are anti-Christian secularists. Far from it; for many UMC persons are Christians, even though the UMC is not the main social basis for Christianity. What I mean to say goes the other way around: I mean that all—or at least *almost* all—anti-Christian secularists are of UMC status.[82] Anti-Christian secularism may not be the *only* ideology found among America's upper-middle class. But it *is* found in this class, and almost exclusively in this class. Secularism's believers and evangelists come from this class, and the ideology is rarely found anywhere else except for two cases. (1) It is sometimes found among very rich people whose socio-economic

---

[82] This is analogous to saying that, while not all Muslims are terrorists, almost all terrorists are Muslims.

standing is higher than mere UMC. Such people, while small in number, are able to make immense financial contributions to the secularist cause. (2) The ideology is also found among some members of classes inferior to the UMC, when these people have been successfully evangelized by UMC secularists. In the case of these lower-middle and working class converts, their secularism is mostly of a passive variety; that is, they believe in abortion, same-sex marriage, etc., but they are not activist crusaders or financial contributors. Yet not many anti-Christian secularists, not even passive secularists, are found among the lower-middle classes, and an even smaller number is found among the working classes. Many persons, especially young persons, of the inferior classes are willing enough to profit from the "benefits" of secularism, e.g., the freedom to fornicate, to cohabit, and to have abortions. But they do so without being aware that in doing this they are repudiating Christianity; they often count themselves as Christian believers, even though they may not be especially active in any church. If they were more intellectually alert and logically consistent, they would realize that they ought to embrace an anti-Christian ideology. But they are non-ideological. They want their sexual freedom, and at the same time they often look forward to meeting Jesus in the next world. But persons of UMC standing tend to be intellectually alert and logically consistent. And so it is not surprising that they understand the connection between an ethic of sexual freedom and a repudiation of Christianity.

It is these inferior classes, the lower-middle and working classes, who provide the principal social base for Christianity, supplemented by many UMC persons who find secularism philosophically unappetizing. As for the lowest classes of all (i.e., those who are downright poor, and permanently so), if they have any ideology at all it is Christianity, which gives them something to hope for in a world in which they don't have many bright worldly hopes.

If the list given above names the social characteristics of the UMC generally, below are the moral-political characteristics of those members of the UMC who are secularist.

- When it comes to questions of the environment, they are decidedly "green."
- They abhor violence. They especially abhor torture.

- They tend to be public policy pacifists. That is, while not absolutely opposed to all war,[83] they think that very little warfare is justifiable. They believe that diplomacy and negotiation and working through the United Nations can, if done sincerely, seriously, and patiently, settle almost all of America's international problem.

- They are very tolerant of people and ideas different from their own. There is one exception however to their tolerance: they are intolerant of intolerance. This explains the negative attitude they have toward religious and moral conservatives, whom they regard as prone to intolerance.

- They are strongly opposed to racism, which they consider to be America's most basic failing.[84]

- They are strongly opposed to homophobia (irrational hatred of homosexual persons) and they believe that almost all opposition to homosexuality and same-sex marriage arises from homophobia.

- They are strong believers in "a woman's right to choose." This doesn't mean that every UMC secularist (if a woman) would feel free to have an abortion or (if a man) to assist a woman in having an abortion. Some of them have either moral or aesthetic objections to abortion. But whether they have personal objections or not, almost all of them believe that all women have a *moral* right to abortion, and all of them believe that women should have a *legal* right to abortion. Usually they believe that taxpayer money should pay for abortions, at least for women who fall below the poverty line.

---

[83] They think, for example, that the American Civil War and World War II were justified, and at least for a while they thought that George Bush's war in Afghanistan was justified. Or perhaps they only pretended to think that the war in Afghanistan was justified; for by saying that that war was justified (a "necessary war") they were better able to denounce Bush's war in Iraq (a "war of choice").

[84] But, as noted above, they are not so strongly opposed as to be willing to send their kids to public schools that contain large numbers of minority children. Nor are they generally willing to see taxpayer money spent to provide poor minority parents with school vouchers, so that these parents too may send their children to private schools.

- They believe in sexual freedom for unmarried persons—but only when combined with prudence and respect for others. Sex should be prudent; that is, when having sex, one should take precautions against unwanted pregnancy and disease. And sex should be respectful; that is, it should not be exploitive or coercive or semi-coercive. They deplore rape and any kind of "nonconsensual" sex, that is, sexual intercourse that takes place without the woman (or girl) giving her full consent.
- They believe that the old idea of premarital chastity is absurd. Young people, beginning in their teen years, *will* have sex and *should* have sex; it's a natural part of the growing-up process. But teens should have a sex education, both at home and at school and via the mass media, that will teach them the importance of sexual prudence and respect. This teaching should include information about contraception and abortion. It should also include lessons on how homosexuality as well as bisexuality and transgenderism are natural and morally legitimate options for some persons.
- They are great believers in embryonic stem-cell research, which they believe has the potential to cure all sorts of maladies; and they strongly favor government funding, at both state and the federal levels, for such research.
- They are far more likely to vote Democratic than Republican, especially in elections for President, US Senate, and US House of Representatives.

How a small secularist minority has won cultural dominance

Granted all the above, it can be pointed out by those who wish to discourage Christian alarmism that the UMC is only a relatively small fraction of American society, less than ten percent. And of that less than ten percent, those UMC people who embrace, even in moderate form, the ideology of anti-Christian secularism are only a fraction of a fraction, probably far less than 50 percent of all UMC people. So let's do the arithmetic. If the United

States has a population of somewhat more than 300 million people, and fewer than 10 percent are upper-middle class, that gives us, let's say, 20 or 25 million people. And if less—very probably much less—than 50 percent of that 20 million are secularists, that leaves us with something between 5 and 10 million. And of that number, a few million are not yet adults. So we are left with, let's say, 3 to 6 million UMC secularists. And that's a generous estimate. Further, in the Culture War the UMC secularists who really count are those who are activists. How many of these are there? Let's say a million or two at most. These numbers of course are no more than guesses (well-educated guesses, I hope). Whatever the precise numbers, however, activists in the secularist cause make up no more than a very small fraction of the US population.

And so the question becomes: How can a few million people out of 300-plus million have a powerful impact on society? How can such a small fraction of the entire population be a serious danger to Catholicism and other traditional forms of Christianity? How can their influence challenge, and in many ways equal or surpass, the influence of the vastly larger pro-Christianity lower-middle and working classes?

Let me tell you how.

1. Numbers. For one thing, as a relative number, a few million may not be many out of a population of 300 million. But as an absolute number, a few million people are a lot of people. An army of a few million could easily subdue a civilian population of 300 million.

2. Money. For another, it's not just a question of numbers. It's also a question of money. Money talks. Not only do UMC secularists have higher average levels of wealth and income than the inferior social classes, that is, the relatively pro-Christianity classes; more important, they have even higher levels of "excess" incomes. That is to say, after Christian believers from the lower-middle and working classes have paid the rent or mortgage, paid the grocery bills, paid for gas, paid the utilities, paid for clothes for themselves and their kids, etc., they don't have much money left over. And of the money they do have left over, much of it goes as a contribution to their church. At the end of the day, they don't have much left to contribute to organizations (other than the church) that are fighting the Culture War in defense of Christian beliefs and values. By contrast, UMC secularists, after they have paid for all the necessities and near-necessities of life, have lots of money left over. This is all the more true since they rarely or never go to church. They can afford to contribute generously to secularist organizations that are fighting the Culture War against Christian beliefs and values. For a lower-middle or working class Christian, it is a genuine sacrifice to send a hundred dollars to, say, the National Right to Life Committee. For a UMC secularist, a thousand-dollar contribution to, say, Planned Parenthood is little more than a drop in the bucket.

3. Organization. And it's not just a question of numbers plus money. The ability to organize and to "network" is important too; and UMC people are much better at this than people from lower social classes. UMC people commonly occupy leadership positions at work and in the community. They are in the habit of mobilizing others in pursuit of long-term or short-term goals; they are in the habit of throwing together ad hoc working groups to deal with this problem or that; they are personally acquainted with many of the movers and shakers of their city and state; and so on. When it comes to fighting the Culture War, UMC secularists can use these contacts and well-developed organizational skills. By contrast, people from the lower-middle class much more rarely occupy important leadership positions and are correspondingly less able to develop organizational skills; and people from the working class almost never occupy leadership positions. Besides, people from these inferior classes rarely have a personal relationship with city-level or state-level movers and shakers.

4. Command posts. Again, UMC secularists dominate what may be called the "command posts" of American culture. More particularly, they dominate three critical command posts: the mainstream media, the entertainment industry, and the nation's high-prestige colleges and universities (including law schools). In these command posts they are well-positioned to disseminate secularist beliefs and values to the American people generally. When it comes to secularization, these command posts have two chief tasks: one is to convert the young to the secularist faith, the other is to confirm older persons in the faith. The entertainment industry (Hollywood and the producers of popular music) reaches the largest number of people, including almost all young people regardless of social class. Elite colleges and universities (Harvard, Yale, Stanford, Berkeley, Michigan, etc.) indoctrinate[85] those who within a few years will be full-fledged members of the UMC. Equally important, they provide the intellectual training needed by those who in the future will be the most articulate makers and defenders of the secularist ideology. The New York Times is an especially interesting case. It is written and edited with a UMC readership chiefly in mind, and its beliefs and values—which are especially found on its editorial pages, but are not restricted to those pages—are decidedly secularist. Moreover the influence of the Times extends far beyond its immediate readership, since other members of the mainstream media commonly take their cue as to news and opinion from the Times.

5. Quasi-secularists. Finally, it's not just a question of outright or full-fledged secularists. Everywhere and in almost all circumstances secularists are supported and aided by quasi-secularists: I mean liberal Christians who attempt, as I've said again and again in this book, to blend—quite incoherently—secularism with Christianity. In almost all Culture War battles between secularists and old-fashioned Christians (battles about abortion, homosexuality, same-sex marriage, embryonic stem-cell research, pornography, sex education, the teaching of the Darwinian theory of evolution in schools, etc.), liberal Christians can be counted on to be on the side of the secularists. The relationship between secularists and liberal Christians (quasi-secularists) is like the old relationship of the 1930s and '40s between "red" Communists and their "pink" leftist-but-non-Communist fellow-travelers. In this latter relationship the Reds supplied most of the ideas and active leadership, while the Pinks supplied numbers and a certain degree of respectability.[86] So it is

---

[85]   This indoctrination, it should be noted, is not mainly carried on by professors lecturing in classrooms, as many cultural conservatives believe. No, it is mainly transacted on a student-to-student basis. If you're a Catholic going to Harvard, you may lose your religious faith, but if so it will probably not be because of your secularist professors. It will be because of your secularist fellow-students.

[86]   The 1948 campaign of Henry Wallace for president is a case in point. Members of the US Communist Party played key leadership roles in the campaign, but the great bulk of Wallace supporters were leftist non-Communists.

in the analogous relationship between secularists and liberal Christians. The ideas and much of the effective leadership come from secularists, but liberal Christians can be relied upon to follow along. In the old days Pinks were often called the "dupes" of the Reds—because the Reds, it was said, if they were to take over the country with the aid of the Pinks, would soon extinguish values of political and personal freedom important to most Pinks; indeed they might well extinguish the Pinks themselves. In the same way today's liberal Christians may be called dupes of secularists—for if secularism, thanks to the aid provided by liberal Christianity, comes to prevail in American culture, it will soon extinguish even the remnants of Christianity that survive among liberal Christians.

Even in a huge country of 300 million people, a mass of a few million, then, is nothing to sneeze at. Add money to these numbers plus organizational skills plus domination of the command posts of American culture plus the aid of liberal Christians, and you see that a few million active secularists can be more than a match for nearly 300 million relatively inert non-secularists.

Inert and Leaderless Catholics

Among these 300 million Americans who are not activists on behalf of anti-Christian secularism, there are about 75 million Catholics—if we take the usual estimate that Catholics make up about 25 percent of the US population.[87] And if these Catholics are relatively inert—which they are—this is in no small measure due to the inertia of you, their bishops. Why have you been inert as

---

[87] But is this 25 percent estimate accurate? It depends on whether we are counting "nominal" plus "real" Catholics or only the latter. By a "real" Catholic here I mean a Catholic who is an active churchgoer, i.e., somebody who attends Mass every (or almost every) weekend. By a "nominal" Catholic I mean a person who, though baptized and perhaps brought up Catholic, has pretty much abandoned his religion (even though in the back of his mind he may have plans to return to it shortly before his death), but has not yet either joined some other religion or told the bishop to remove his name from the rolls. Probably nominal Catholics now outnumber real Catholics in America.

---

the anti-Christian crusade made great advances during the past 40 or 50 years? A look at the history of the episcopacy may provide us with the clue needed to answer this question. For many centuries, the great majority of Catholic bishops were found in Catholic countries, that is, countries in which almost everybody was a Catholic. And so, if you became a bishop, you had to do little more than mind the store. You didn't have to spread the faith, for it had already spread to everybody. Nor did you have to defend the faith from its enemies, for it had hardly any serious enemies. All you had to do, with the assistance of your diocesan clergy, was to say Mass, administer the sacraments, and preach the Gospel to the already converted; in other words, while minding the store, you had to provide good service to your customers. In using this expression ("minding the store"), I don't mean to minimize the importance or even the difficulty of being a minding-the-store kind of bishop. Creating a flourishing business is one thing; maintaining it once it has achieved success is another. The latter is a lesser achievement than the former, but it is a nonetheless notable achievement.

The United States was of course never a Catholic society, but up until the 1960s American Catholics lived, as I noted earlier in the book, within a quasi-ghetto; American Catholicism had become, in a way, a society within a society, a kind of *imperium in imperio*. Once the "ghetto" had been established, American bishops could adopt the minding-the-store attitude that in those days would have been appropriate for a bishop in, say, Portugal or Ireland. But that age is now long past.[88] Beginning about 50 years ago, Catholicism (along with old-fashioned Protestantism) came under tremendous attack; it was as if a gang of thieves had broken into the store. But you bishops, I am sorry to say, acted as if you didn't notice the burglars. You didn't embark upon a vigorous campaign to repulse the attack; and you certainly didn't go out into the highways and byways to convert people to Christianity. You just kept on pretending to mind the store, and many of you still have this attitude. No wonder a few million secularists have been able to out-think, out-maneuver, and out-gun tens of millions of Catholics—that is to say, tens of millions of *relatively leaderless Catholics*.

---

[88] Not just in the United States but in Ireland and Portugal too.

It must be kept in mind that in the social world of Catholicism only bishops—let me repeat: *only bishops*—can provide effective leadership. There are some exceptions to this rule, but not many. Every so often a charismatic non-bishop—Francis of Assisi, for instance—appears on the scene and develops a tremendous following. But in the normal course of affairs, it is bishops who provide leadership for Catholics. This has usually been a great strength among Catholics, this readiness among lay Catholics to follow their episcopal leaders and not to follow anybody else. For when a bishop spoke, you knew he wasn't speaking just for himself; he was speaking for a very large number of loyal followers. And you also knew that the authority of the bishop could not effectively be challenged by any dissident group within the Church. But when bishops fall down on the job, when they fail to provide the leadership needed at a particular critical moment in history, this "great strength" can become a great weakness. Before acting, rank-and-file Catholics wait for a signal from their bishops; when no signal is given, these Catholics do not act; like their bishops, they sit on their hands. For decades now we have been living through one of these critical historical moments, and you bishops have on the whole failed to provide the needed leadership. The laity, lacking episcopal leadership, does little or nothing to fight back against the anti-Christian crusade—and when I refer to the laity here I have in mind the "real Catholic" laity, not merely the "nominal Catholic" laity. The latter of course won't fight against secularism; on the contrary, they assist the enemies of Catholicism.

The Catholic community, it must be remembered, is not like the Jewish community. Among Jews, rabbis play an important leadership role, but they have no monopoly on leadership. Jewish laypersons—including at times lay Jews who are almost thoroughly nonreligious—also play important leadership roles; indeed they usually play a far more important leadership role than do the rabbis, for instance in the support given by American Jews to Israel. There is nothing like this in Catholicism. For better or worse the Catholic Church is structured in such a way that bishops, not laypersons, are the leaders. So if you bishops don't lead, we are leaderless; and if you lead poorly, then we have poor leadership; and if we have no leadership or poor leadership, then by and large we laypersons don't act.

The Democratic Party

But it gets worse. Not only do UMC secularists dominate the command posts of American culture; they also dominate one of the nation's two great political parties. The national Democratic Party is today largely in the hands of anti-Christian secularists. This is not true of all state-level or big-city Democratic parties, although it is true of many of them, perhaps even most. And it is even less true of small-town Democratic parties, many of which remain controlled by old-fashioned Catholics or Protestants. But at the *national* level the Democratic Party has become—let us face facts—an anti-Christian party.[89] It now bears little resemblance to the party it was in the days of, say, Franklin Roosevelt and Harry Truman and John Kennedy. In its hostility to Christianity, especially Catholicism, it is less like the Democratic Party of yore and more like the leftwing anti-Catholic parties of France's Third Republic.

When I say this I don't mean that the average Democratic voter is anti-Christian. Not only is this not the case; it is the opposite of the case. The average Democratic voter—e.g., the labor union member, the African-American, the Latino—is usually a Christian, often a Catholic. For the most part these voters are unaware, or only barely aware, of the secularist, anti-Christian nature of today's party. Many of them, especially those who are old enough to have voted for John Kennedy (1960) or even Harry Truman (1948), fall into the fallacy of "essentialism" when thinking about politics. That is, they feel that political parties, like geometrical shapes, have eternal and unchanging essences. Once a triangle has three sides, it will always have three sides; and once the Democratic Party has the benign characteristics it had in the days of FDR and Truman and Kennedy, it will always have these characteristics. "If the Democratic Party wasn't an anti-Christian party 50 or 60 or 70 years ago, it can't possibly be an anti-Christian party today"—so runs the thinking of older Democrats who have fallen into the essentialist fallacy.

---

[89]   For a detailed account of this, see my book, *Can a Catholic Be a Democrat?* (Sophia Institute Press, 2006).

Further, there are Democratic Catholic voters who are sometimes made a bit uncomfortable by the pro-abortion and pro-homosexuality positions taken by many leading Democratic politicians; but these feelings of discomfort are outweighed by the conviction that the Democratic Party will support the racial and/or economic interests of Democratic voters. These voters say to themselves, "Yes, I know the Democratic Party has a number of imperfections. But nobody's perfect. And the good points of the party far outweigh its bad points—not to mention that the alternative to the Democrats is the Republicans, who are still as awful as ever, if not worse." Besides, most average Democratic voters don't "connect the dots"—they don't perceive these pro-abortion and pro-homosexuality policies as part of a larger secularist, anti-Christian agenda. For them, there is a veil that conceals the real nature of today's Democratic Party.

What's more, Democratic politicians work to keep this veil in place. Many of these politicians don't like to admit to themselves that the party has changed radically since the days of their parents and grandparents. As a result, they practice the same kind of selective ignorance that is engaged in by the voters I have just spoken of. They too imagine that their party is still at heart the party of FDR, Truman, and Kennedy, albeit with a few moral liberals operating at the margins. Besides, all Democratic politicians, even those who are themselves fully committed anti-Christian secularists, realize that it won't do to remind the average voter of the party's commitment to abortion and same-sex marriage. And so, except when running in a very liberal district (e.g., some university town) or addressing a select and very liberal audience (e.g., a fund-raising crowd made up of supporters of Planned Parenthood or the ACLU), these politicians minimize their emphasis on abortion and homosexuality, and concentrate instead on Social Security, health care for all, public education, growing the economy, etc.

And when I say that today's Democratic Party is dominated by anti-Christian secularists, I don't mean to say that there are no other important "players" in the party. The labor unions are still players, and so are organized African-Americans; and neither group is committed to anti-Christianity; indeed blacks tend to be strongly pro-Christianity. But increasingly these two become players of secondary roles only; increasingly secularists take the starring role. And as long as secularists take care of—or at least pretend to take care of—the interests of labor and blacks, labor and blacks do not resist the anti-Christian agenda of the secularists who are dominant in the party.

Nor do I mean that all national-level Democratic politicians—members, for instance, of the United States Senate and House of Representatives—are themselves anti-Christian secularists. Not at all. For the most part these politicians are Christians; often they are Catholic; in some cases (but probably not an awful lot of cases) they are even pious Catholics. But if they wish to win office and remain in office, they have to keep their key backers happy, backers who have money and social influence; and these key backers are frequently secularists; and politicians keep these well-to-do and influential secularists happy by supporting their agenda, or at least by not opposing it.

Julius Caesar once said that money is the "sinews of war," and it is certainly the sinews of American politics. And it is more than just the sinews: it supplies the muscles and bones and blood as well. Time was when money didn't count as much in politics as it does now. In the old days (back in the time of FDR and Truman), local and state political parties ("machines") counted. The national party stood at the apex of a pyramid, at the base of which were the local parties, and in between the base and the apex were the state parties. The national party got its message out by relying on the state parties, which in turn relied on local parties. But the age of state and local political machines is, with only a few exceptions (Chicago, for instance), gone. For decades now the national party and its candidates have relied on television advertising to get their message out, and TV advertising is, as everybody knows, expensive—phenomenally expensive, both for the purchase of air time and for production costs. Hence national candidates are dependent above all on people who have money to contribute to political campaigns. And as everybody has always known: *He who pays the piper calls the tune.* Increasingly too the Internet has come to play an important role in major political campaigns, partly because of webpage propaganda, partly because of online fundraising, and partly because of online paid advertising. All this too favors the affluent and well-educated sectors of the Democratic Party, that is, the secularist sectors of the party. For they have the cleverness needed to utilize the Internet to maximum advantage, and they have the spare change needed to make Internet political contributions.

And it's not simply a question of money. Given their dominance of the command posts of culture (national press, entertainment industry, colleges and universities), secularists can help or hurt political candidates by disseminating a good word or a bad word about them to the general public.

What's more, since these secularist supporters are ideologues, their support for Democratic candidates is, we may say, *contingent*. Their support for a candidate very much depends on whether the candidate takes the "right" stand on crucial issues. These supporters are Democrats, but they are at the opposite end of the spectrum from the "yellow dog" Democrat.[90] If a Democrat takes the "wrong" stand, these ideologues are willing to vote for a Republican who takes the "right" stand; or they are willing to abstain from voting; or in a party primary they will support an alternative Democrat who takes the "right" stand; or they will support any third-party candidate (e.g., Ralph Nader) who runs to the left of the Democratic candidate.

The Obama-for-president campaign was a very striking illustration of all this. In addition to his own remarkable electioneering talents, Barack Obama's successes in 2008 and 2012 were due chiefly to a de facto coalition of two groups, white UMC secularists plus African-Americans.[91] (Talk about politics making for strange bedfellows!) Besides their mutual fondness for Obama, the two have little in common: on the one hand, atheists and agnostics (along of course with their quasi-secularist Christian fellow-travelers); on the other, old-fashioned Christian believers. And this latter group—black Christian voters—had little suspicion that their Democratic Party was largely controlled by a social-cultural group whose ultimate goal is the thoroughgoing de-Christianization of America. At the same time the former group—UMC secularists—realize that, at least for the time being, their cause cannot be

---

[90] A "yellow dog Democrat" is defined as a person who is so strongly committed to the Democratic Party that he will vote for a Democratic candidate no matter how bad the candidate is; he will vote Democratic even if the Democratic candidate is a yellow dog.

[91] Young voters were a third group. But many of the most active pro-Obama campaigners among the young were themselves secularists, ardent supporters of abortion rights and same-sex marriage. So young voters were not so much a distinct third group as they were in large measure a sub-section of one of the other two groups.

represented by a presidential candidate who is fully and openly one of themselves; they will have to be satisfied with a religious believer who supports their agenda of sexual liberalism. As for Obama himself, if he meant to be a viable Democratic candidate for the presidency, he had no choice, even if he is in some sense a sincere Christian, but to embrace policies that are high on the UMC secularist agenda, policies that are quite incompatible with traditional Christian morality. From the UMC secularist point of view, Obama was the ideal candidate: a black Christian (or pretended Christian) who agreed with their agenda. Whether he was sincere in his Christianity or not did not matter to the secularists. If sincere, his Christianity was of the liberal kind—that is, the semi-Christian kind; a kind that secularists consider pretty harmless. And if insincere, so what? In 2008 Obama didn't mean it when he said that he was opposed to same-sex marriage; and most of his secularist supporters realized at the time that he didn't mean it, that he would need time to "evolve" (as he later put it). Likewise maybe he doesn't mean it when he says he is a Christian believer. It really doesn't matter, for the important thing is that he embraces the anti-Christianity agenda of the secularists; there is no need for him to go one step further and say that he is actually opposed to Christianity.

And so, while a certain number of high Democratic elected officials may be outright secularists, the great majority of them are not. Yet because of their need for the financial and other kinds of support that secularists and quasi-secularists (liberal Christians) give, these Christian Democrats are tied to secularism's anti-Christian agenda. Thus they are reliable defenders of the right to abortion. They are proponents of the agenda of the gay movement. And when euthanasia, thanks to secularist pro-euthanasia propaganda, becomes more acceptable than it is now to the general public, these Democratic politicians, it is easy to predict, will turn out to be pro-euthanasia, and will denounce the lack of "compassion" that motivates foes of euthanasia.

It is interesting to see how the position of the typical Democratic politician has evolved on homosexuality issues. The mainstream secularist position on these and other issues is always more "advanced" than the position of Democratic politicians; for the latter, while trying to please their secularist backers, also have to avoid alienating their more traditional supporters.

In other words, these politicians have to tread carefully, inching their way forward, not leaping in one bound to the ultimate goal. And so when it came to gay issues, they first demanded simple fairness, that is, no discrimination in the workplace; next they pushed for open gays in the military; and then they supported "civil unions" (but no marriage) for gays; and finally they have come to support same-sex marriage. Now same-sex marriage was the goal all along, and this was fairly obvious to anybody who was paying careful attention.[92] But cautious Democratic politicians couldn't admit this. They had to pretend that they were interested only in the question immediately before them. Think of how it took Obama years to "evolve." Anybody with a political brain in his head knew where Obama was heading and would finally end up. But Obama couldn't admit this until the time was ripe; till then he had to pretend—that is, to use a plain English word, he had to *lie* to the public—that he was opposed to same-sex marriage. Finally, in mid-2012 the time was ripe, and Obama, telling the truth at last, could finally announce that he was a supporter of same-sex marriage.

I just said that same-sex marriage "was the goal all along." But it was not, and is not, the *ultimate* goal. The further goal (and this still isn't the ultimate goal) is to persuade society that homosexual marriage is morally equivalent to heterosexual marriage; that homosexuality is just as "natural" as heterosexuality; and—except for forcible rape, the seduction of very young children,[93] and cases in which an HIV-infected person proceeds to have sex

---

[92] It was obvious to me, for example, when in 1992, as a member of the Rhode Island Senate, I voted against a "gay rights" bill that would have prohibited discrimination based on sexual orientation. It's not that I was in favor of discrimination or the right to discriminate. But I judged, correctly as it turned out, that this anti-discrimination bill was only incidentally about discrimination. What it was really about was winning the state's stamp of approval for homosexuality, and it would lead to a subsequent demand for same-sex marriage. In 2013, long after I had left the Senate and was no longer available to fight against the proposal in the State House, Rhode Island enacted a same-sex marriage law.

[93] Except for members of NAMBLA (the North American Man-Boy Love Association), everybody in the gay movement would agree that it is wrong to have sex with an "underage" person. But they are far from agreeing on what counts as underage.

without informing his partner of this medical condition—there is nothing morally wrong in *any kind* of homosexual activity, including the most casual and impersonal encounters. Once society is persuaded of all this, then it will also be persuaded (and *this* is the ultimate goal) that Christianity is a profoundly false religion—for there is no way in which one can believe in "all this" and believe in Christianity too.

The challenge

Your battle, then, my dear bishops, is not simply against a system of false opinions, against a "heresy" (an old-fashioned but useful word). No, it is against a socially and politically powerful group of people. Your situation is rather like that of the Catholic/Orthodox bishops during those years of the 4th century when the emperor himself was an Arian. Arianism was not merely a heresy; it was a heresy embraced and endorsed by the most powerful people in the empire. It is not encouraging to remember that most bishops caved in: they were unwilling to fight against Arianism if this meant fighting against the emperor and his friends.[94] But there were a few bishops ready to stand up for their religious convictions, most notably of course the great Athanasius. Is there an Athanasius (or John Fisher) today among you American bishops? There should be scores of them. Can we find even a half-dozen? There are millions of rank-and-file Catholics willing to do battle for the faith. All they lack is leadership. (The hungry sheep look up, and are not fed). A group that lacks leadership, however, lacks everything.

[end of chapter]

---

[94] Nor is it encouraging to remember that all bishops but one—John Fisher of Rochester—caved in when King Henry VIII seized control of the Church in England. As a number of uprisings indicated, the Catholic people of England were ready to fight for their Church. But almost all of their leaders deserted them.

PART TWO

WHAT MUST BE DONE

In this, the second and final part of the book, I shift from diagnosis to prescription. In the first part I gave an account of the nature of the problem that faces American Catholicism (as well as old-fashioned American Christianity in general). In this part I make some practical suggestions as to how you bishops can deal with this problem.

These practical suggestions fall under two general headings.

First, I suggest that American Catholicism needs to make secularism its "official enemy," just as, in the period that began with the Council of Trent in the 16th century, the Catholic Church made Protestantism its official enemy; and just as in the 8th century the Catholic/Orthodox Church made iconoclasm its official enemy; and just as in the 4th century the Catholic/Orthodox Church made Arianism the official enemy. The Church has always had, and very probably always will have, enemies, whether internal or external. And the Church, to judge from history, has its greatest vitality when, drawing a "bright line" between itself and its enemies, it fights to preserve itself.

Second, coming down to brass tacks, I suggest some techniques bishops can use to instruct and mobilize the faithful in this fight for survival.

CHAPTER 8

Drawing Bright Lines

In this chapter and the next (the two final chapters of the book), I will offer some practical advice to you bishops, suggestions as to how you can protect Catholicism in American—and perhaps even help it to thrive once again. I offer this advice however with fear and trembling, since I am no expert on the subject of how to revive declining religions; indeed there probably is no such thing as an expert on this subject. What I offer, even though I'm sincere in my belief that it is good advice, may in the end turn out to be bad advice. I hope not—but *caveat emptor*. An effective plan for saving American Catholicism cannot be laid down in advance. It will have to be discovered experimentally on a trial-and-error basis. But we have to start *somewhere*, and my suggested "somewhere" may be as good as any.

The fundamental principle lying behind all the advice I offer is this, that you bishops have to draw a "bright line" between Catholicism and its present-day enemies—both its clearcut enemy, secularism, and its perhaps more dangerous enemy, that semi-secularist thing that goes by the name of liberal or modernist Christianity. For well over a century liberal Christianity was a deviation from genuine Christianity infecting Protestant churches only.[95] But since the time of Vatican II in the 1960s it has infected the Catholic Church as well.[96]

In the history of Catholicism there have been many enemies of orthodox faith and practice, hence bright lines have been drawn again and again; for it seems that the only way the faith can be preserved when confronted by an enemy is by drawing such bright lines. If they are not drawn, many Catholics will find themselves compromising with the enemy, trying to find a via media that will, they hope, allow both sides to live in peace with one another. This via media will be a middle way between orthodoxy[97] and its heretical foe, and as a result orthodoxy will soon come to be perceived, when viewed from the middle way point of view, as a kind of extremism. If orthodoxy is to be preserved, that is to say, if Catholicism itself is to be preserved, such middle-way strategies have to be avoided or renounced. Catholics have to rally 'round the flag of orthodoxy.

A bright line was drawn against the Judaizers in the time of St. Paul (see especially his Letter to the Galatians). A bright line was drawn in the 4th century against the Arians (remember, my dear bishops, one of the brightest ornaments of your order, your fellow-bishop Athanasius of Alexandria). Bright lines were later drawn against iconoclasts (who were Christians tinged

---

[95]   A kind of liberal Catholicism, going under the name of "Modernism," was found in Catholic circles in the late 19th and early 20th centuries. But it was effectively suppressed by Pope Pius X, and did not trouble the Church again until the 1960s. See Pius's two anti-Modernist documents of 1907: "Lamentabili" (a syllabus of Modernist errors) and "Pascendi" (an encyclical letter on the same topic).

[96]   For an early and strenuous negative reaction to this neo-Modernism, see Jacques Maritain's *The Peasant of the Garonne*. (Published in French in 1966, its English translation appeared in 1968: Holt, Rinehart and Winston.) Up till the publication of this book, Maritain, largely because of his political liberalism, had for 30 years or more been a great favorite of Catholics who thought of themselves as liberal. But when *The Peasant* made them realize that Maritain was, religiously speaking, a very orthodox Catholic, they overnight ceased being his fans. However, anybody who had read him carefully in his pre-*Peasant* years should have realized that Maritain, though a political liberal, was no religious liberal. He had never been anything but a very orthodox Catholic.

[97]   When I say "orthodoxy" here, I mean orthopraxis as well. That is, I am speaking not just of right belief, but of right conduct too.

with Islamic attitudes—not unlike today's liberal Catholics, who are Catholics tinged with secularist attitudes). Coming down to early modern times, only a few centuries ago a bright line—a very, very bright line—was drawn in the period of the so-called Counter-Reformation against Protestantism. The Church of the Counter-Reformation did not attempt to conciliate Protestantism by compromising essential elements of Catholicism in hopes that Protestants would as a result find the old religion less objectionable. If the Church leadership had done that, we would have ended up with a religion that was a halfway compromise between Catholicism and Protestantism; and this via media religion would in effect have been a kind of Protestantism, since it would have deviated from Catholic orthodoxy. Instead of compromising, Counter-Reformation Catholicism did just the opposite. Anything among the essential, or even near-essential, characteristics of Catholicism that Protestants objected to, Rome re-affirmed. Did Protestants object to the papacy? Well, then, papal domination of the Church would be stressed more than ever. Did Protestants object to the cults of the Virgin and the saints? Well, let's have more of the Virgin and the saints. Did Protestants object to convents and monasteries? Let's have nuns and monks galore. Did Protestants object to the Real Presence of Christ in the Eucharist? Well, let's underline the transubstantiation theory of the Real Presence. Did Protestants, or at least its more puritanical wing, object to fancy churches with paintings, statues, stained glass windows, burning candles, and so on? Well, let's have more of these than ever: let's have baroque architecture and interior design. To this day a visitor to Rome will notice the city's abundance of baroque churches, not just baroque churches that were built that way from the ground up, but older churches that were re-designed and re-decorated in a baroque manner. This was Rome's way of saying, "Make no mistake about it: we are a Catholic city, not a Protestant city—and, God save the mark, not a Puritan city."

Drawing bright lines makes it clear to everybody, both our own people and those sympathetic to the enemy, that there is a real difference between the two camps, and it clarifies the nature of that difference. More, it forces people to choose sides by eliminating the foggy middle ground that has hitherto lain between us and the enemy, a foggy middle that is attractive both to the religiously lukewarm and to those who don't quite like orthodoxy. By drawing a bright line, you say to the lukewarm: "Are you with Catholicism or with its foes? Choose!" Forcing this choice, of course, will drive many of the lukewarm out of the Church. But it will drive many others to embrace the Church in a whole-hearted way, and there will very probably be more of the latter than of the former. Why so? Because the foggy middle ground is comfortable territory for the lukewarm, but when the foggy middle disappears, and the lukewarm Catholic is offered the alternative of Catholicism or outright secularism, he will usually choose Catholicism. He may have objections to full-fledged Catholicism, but his objections to full-fledged secularism are even greater. His situation is like that of a young man who has been cohabiting for a few years with his girlfriend, until one day she, having grown impatient, offers him this alternative: "Marry me, or the affair is finished." Now many young men find that the cohabitation arrangement suits their lukewarmness: it gives them many of the benefits of marriage (companionship, regular sex, home-cooked meals) without the onus of permanent commitment. But faced with the girlfriend's ultimatum, young men usually decide (after pulling a long face of course) to marry. For, unattractive as marriage may be, for most of them the alternative is even worse.

In this chapter I will discuss the *content* of the bright line that needs to be drawn between Catholicism and secularism (along with its fellow-traveler, liberal Christianity). That is, I will indicate the issues that divide, or ought to divide, the two sides. In the next chapter I will make some suggestions regarding techniques, that is, suggestions as to the devices you bishops can use to communicate with and to mobilize your own people about these issues.

The Four Elements of Catholicism

Catholicism, like any religion, contains three essential elements:

- Doctrine
- Ritual
- Morality

In the case of Catholicism, and more so here than in almost any other religion, a fourth element is also of great importance:

• Church polity or government.

An anti-secularist Catholicism, a Catholicism that draws a bright line between itself and secularism, will therefore have to be anti-secularist in all four dimensions: doctrine, ritual, morals, and polity. It will have to draw bright lines at all four places.

It would be convenient at this stage in my argument to be able to paint a picture of what, in all four dimensions, this anti-secularist Catholicism would look like. The trouble is that nobody—and certainly not I—knows how to draw accurate pictures of the human future. It is hard enough to predict tomorrow's weather, never mind predicting what vast numbers of human beings will do over the next century or two. If American Catholicism is to take on an anti-secularist form, this form will have to be *discovered* on an experimental basis over an extended period of time. Things will have to be tried out, retained if they work, discarded if they don't work, until American Catholicism finally achieves a viable anti-secularist form. It will not be the work of a summer's day. Above all, it will not be the work of an architect who lays down *a priori* plans.

What a surviving Church will *not* look like

While it may be difficult or impossible to say what a surviving and flourishing Catholic Church in American will look like, it relatively easy to say a few things about what it will *not* look like.

1. Not a ghetto. For one, it will not be the "ghetto" church that existed prior to the 1960s. Even if it were desirable to return to this earlier era, this could not be done. The hands on the clock of history do not run backwards. Catholics have been out of their quasi-ghetto for more than a half-century now. They are fully part of the mainstream of American life. There is no going back.

2. Not a sect. Again, it will not be a sect, that is, a small and socially isolated group of believers who are full of high-intensity religion, e.g.,

Jehovah's Witnesses. Catholicism, for better or worse, has always been a "mixed" religion, composed of a minority of high-intensity believers plus a great majority of relatively low-intensity believers. It is a religion that is never content to be small and selective. Nor is Catholicism, which holds itself to be a religion made for the entire human race, comfortable being a "closed" society, cut off from contact with the outside world.

3. Not a denomination. Nor will it be a standard American "denomination" akin to the mainline Protestant churches, e.g., Episcopal, Methodist, Presbyterian, Evangelical Lutheran Church of America, or the United Church of Christ. At the present moment, it is true, the Catholic Church in the United States is in actual practice pretty much a denomination of this kind. And so, like the mainline Protestant churches, it is in a state of decline; for this is what happens to standard American denominations—they go into decline. The essential mark of denominational churches is their theological tolerance: their adherents tend to believe that all religions are approximately as good as one another. But if all religions are as good as one another, it really doesn't matter which one you belong to; and it is only one small step further to the conclusion that it really doesn't matter whether or not you belong to any religion at all. For a few decades now Catholics in the United States have been "tolerant" (that is, indifferent) in a denominational kind of way; they have had what may be called a "denominational mentality."[98] But this has led to a decline of Catholicism in America. Thus if Catholicism is to have a future in this country, it will have to eliminate its tendency to be a religion of the denominational kind. It will have to be a theologically "intolerant" religion. In other words, it will have to recover and re-assert its essentially intolerant nature. A religion that claims to be the "true" religion of God cannot afford to be indifferent to theological error. It cannot afford to say, "We have the truth, but your error is just as good as our truth." I stress, however, that I'm speaking of *theological* intolerance, not social or legal intolerance. There must be no interference with the right of conscience—a right that includes the right to be in error.

---

[98]   For a fuller treatment of the idea of a denominational mentality, see chapters 13 through 19 of my book, *The Decline and Fall of the Catholic Church in America.*

4. Not a national religion. It will not become the universal religion of the United States, with virtually all Americans joining the Catholic Church, just as for many centuries virtually everybody in many European or Latin American countries was Catholic. Religious pluralism has always been, and no doubt will always be, an essential characteristic of American society and culture.

5. A fifth form. If Catholicism is to survive and flourish in the United States, and if this Catholicism of the future will not take any of the four forms listed above, it will have to take a fifth form. Rather, it will have to *discover* a fifth form. Historically speaking, Christian religions—Catholic, Orthodox, and Protestant—have taken one or more of the four forms just outlined. Hence a fifth form will be a *new* form, one that nobody has seen up till now.

The positive characteristics of an anti-secularist church

One thing that can be said, however, is that this new form of Church will have to be anti-secularist. That being the case, this new thing, this fifth form, will almost certainly have to stress certain key propositions if it is to be anti-secularist in a bright-line kind of way. What follows here is a list of some—but probably not all—of these key propositions.

1. Pertaining to knowledge:

(a) Faith as cognitive. Since secularism insists that religious faith is nothing more than a man-made construct grounded in a combination of emotion and imagination, having no cognitive value, Catholics will have to affirm the contrary, that faith *does* have cognitive value, that it is a genuine form of knowledge. They will have to insist that the person of faith, other things being equal, knows more about reality than does the unbeliever; that the person of faith, in other words, is more of a realist than is the atheist/agnostic.

(b) Communication with God. Catholicism has always held that prayer can be a two-way street. In prayer it is not just that we communicate with God, but God often communicates with us as well. This is especially true in mystical experience, the highest and most intense form of prayer, in which (mystics tell us) the soul of the mystic enters into a kind of union with God. This union with the divine is a union of love, but it is also a union of knowledge. The mystic comes away from the experience with more wisdom than he or she had going into it; the mystic has acquired a personal and intimate knowledge of God that the rest of us lack. And what is true of mysticism is true to a lesser degree of other forms—lesser forms—of religious experience, namely, that they involve a communication from God, that the religious person comes away from this experience knowing something about God that he/she did not know beforehand.[99]

Secularists need not deny that "religious experiences" take place. What they deny is that the experiences have objective validity, that they give knowledge of some reality outside the mind of the person undergoing the experience. Instead they are purely *subjective* experiences, purely psychological phenomena. Religious people often *feel* they have received a communication from God, the secularist will concede, but this is no evidence that they *actually have* received such a communication. After all, in certain mental institutions there are people who sincerely *feel* they are Napoleon, but this is no evidence that they really *are* Napoleon.

Catholicism has never held that every claim to a mystical or near-mystical or semi-mystical religious experience is valid. It can freely admit that some of these claims are innocent mistakes, some self-delusions, some psychopathic delusions, and so forth. Thus it can go a long way with secularists in their dismissal of religious experience claims. But it cannot go all the way, for that would be tantamount to denying that God has the power to communicate with individuals; or at least it would be tantamount to affirming that God, notwithstanding his capacities, has a strict policy of non-communication. But both of these propositions would be absurd from the point of view of the Catholic faith. Hence Catholicism holds that God *can* communicate with

---

[99] This knowledge will not to any notable degree be propositional knowledge, that is, knowledge that can be expressed in clear and distinct concepts.

individuals in a religious experience; and furthermore, that from time to time God actually *does* communicate with individuals.

(c) Moral knowledge. Most secularists, though perhaps not all, hold that moral codes and values are, in the last analysis, no more than cultural constructs or personal choices/preferences.[100] Catholics, therefore, heirs to the Natural Law theory of the ancient Stoics and Cicero, have to insist that there is such a thing as moral *knowledge*; that ethical propositions are either true or false; that the human mind is capable of recognizing a moral law that is objective and not man-made.

(d) Intelligibility of reality. Contemporary American secularism has a powerful bias toward skepticism, not just religious and moral skepticism, but skepticism of a more generalized kind, often designated by that multi-purpose word "postmodernism." As heir to the great schools of classical philosophy (Plato and Aristotle), Catholics have to insist that the human intellect is proportioned to the objective world, that the intellect is capable of grasping reality. Ironically, Catholicism, which has often been charged by its foes with being the enemy of modern scientific knowledge (e.g., the case of Galileo, which is endlessly thrown in the face of the Church), now has the duty of defending the possibility of knowledge, including scientific knowledge, against the skeptics.

(e) Provability of the existence of God. The First Vatican Council taught that it is possible to prove, by means of natural reason alone (that is, without borrowing any premises from Divine Revelation), that God exists; however, it did not endorse any particular proof (or proofs) of God's existence. In effect, then, the Council was saying: "There is at least one rational proof of God's existence, but we're not telling you what it is"—analogous to saying: "There is a treasure buried on this island, but we won't tell you where precisely." Catholic philosophers and theologians should take this as a challenge; they should go looking for this treasure. They might find it by means of newly discovered proofs, or they might find it by re-examining old proofs, e.g., those of Augustine or

---

[100] It should be recognized, however, that these secularists, despite their theory that the rules of morality are either social or individual constructs, often talk and act as though certain rules of morality have objective validity, e.g., "Thou shalt not be a racist," "Thou shalt not be a sexist," "Thou shalt not be homophobic," and "Thou shalt not contribute to global warming."

Anselm or Aquinas. By offering and defending such proofs, they are drawing the clearest possible contrast between Catholicism and secularism. They are saying: "You secularists deny the existence of God; we by contrast not only affirm that existence, but we'll prove it to you." In doing this, however, Catholics have to be careful to avoid fallacious—or at least obviously fallacious—"proofs." For offering such "proofs" brings discredit to the entire Catholic enterprise.

2. Pertaining to metaphysical reality:

(a) **Theism.** Secularism is either atheistic or agnostic; moreover, this agnosticism is usually a *de facto* atheism. Therefore Catholics will have to put special stress on their belief in God. In the long anti-Protestant era, from Trent until Vatican II, there was no need to stress this fundamental belief (the most fundamental of all Christian beliefs), since it was not a point of disagreement between Catholics and Protestants. But in the new anti-secularist era, this is the principal point of differentiation between Catholics and their rivals.

Such an emphasis will produce two incidental benefits. First, it will highlight what Catholicism has in common with other religions, especially other Christian faiths (Protestantism and the Eastern Orthodox churches), thus making it easier to join these other Christian faiths in a great Christian alliance against secularism, and even to join non-Christian faiths (especially Judaism and Islam) in a great monotheistic alliance. Second, more attention to the idea of God will lead to a deeper understanding of that idea, not just at the level of theology and philosophy, but, perhaps more importantly, at the level of popular belief.

(b) **Life after death.** From a secularist point of view, belief in life after death makes little or no sense. Thus Catholics, in order to draw a very sharp line of distinction between themselves and secularists, must stress this belief. All the considerations just mentioned with regard to belief in the existence of God apply here as well.

(c) **Grace and free will.** Secularism has embraced modern psychology and sociology, in both their scholarly and "pop" versions; and according to the usual understanding of these social sciences, human behavior is totally explainable, at least in principle, in naturalistic terms. Explanations of human behavior in terms of supernatural forces—the grace of God—are ruled out of court; and explanations in terms of free will are ruled out as well (for free will, if not exactly a supernatural force, is not a "natural" force either). As against secularism, Catholicism has to stress that grace and free will play important roles in human conduct. This will be a very ticklish undertaking, since, while asserting the reality of grace and free will, Catholicism will have to abstain from a wholesale rejection of psychology and sociology—although it will of course have to reject the naturalistic and deterministic framework that typically lies in the deep background of these behavioral sciences. This probably means that Catholic social scientists and philosophers will have to develop specifically Christian versions of psychology and sociology.

3. Pertaining to morality

(a) **Moral law.** Above I argued for the need to affirm the *knowledge* of an objective moral law, and this entails of course the need to affirm the *existence* of this law. Secularists usually hold that the rules of morality are purely man-made things, either societal and cultural products or the creations of individuals. Hence Catholicism has to emphasize the diametric opposite, that there is a moral law that is not man-made, a God-made—or at least a God-*based*—law.[101] In addition to this fundamental law of morality, of course,

---

[101] To speak of the moral law as "God-made," while acceptable at the level of popular discourse, especially discourse involving children and poorly educated adults, is philosophically misleading. Why? Because it suggests that the moral law is the product of God's arbitrary will; from which it would follow that lying, cheating, stealing, adultery, murder, etc., while wrong today, would be right tomorrow if God were to change his mind. Although this is what some Catholic theologians (e.g., William of Occam in the 14th century) have had in mind, this is not what the main current of Catholic theology and philosophy has held. Thomas Aquinas and others have held that the moral law is ultimately based on God, but not on God's will so much as on his reason; and more immediately the moral law is based on the rational nature of the human person. See Aquinas, *Summa Theologica*, I-II, question 90.

there may also be many man-made laws. But these man-made laws must either be derivable from the fundamental laws or at least not incompatible with them.

(b) Abortion, suicide, euthanasia. For decades now American secularism has found nothing morally objectionable in abortion; for the most part it finds nothing morally objectionable in suicide; and increasingly it finds nothing morally objectionable in euthanasia, especially voluntary euthanasia. And given the principle of moral liberalism, logic dictates that even *involuntary* euthanasia is unobjectionable in cases in which the victim would be "better off" dead but lacks the capacity to make this decision. Catholicism, therefore, in drawing bright lines between itself and its foe must emphasize in the strongest possible terms the Catholic opposition to abortion, suicide, and euthanasia.

For the time being at least, secularism is more attached to the imaginary "right to abortion" than it is to any imaginary rights to suicide or euthanasia. This means that the Church, in drawing bright lines, has to pay more attention, at least for the time being, to abortion than to suicide or euthanasia. More perhaps than anything else, it has been abortion that secularism has used to undermine and destroy Christianity in America during the last half-century. The sexual revolution generally has served to undermine and destroy Christianity, but in that process abortion has been the single most important element—the keystone in the arch, so to speak. And this for two reasons. First, without abortion there could be no real sexual revolution, or at most it would have been no more than a mild revolution. For in a culture of sexual freedom, "mistakes" will inevitably be made from time to time, even when people generally take contraceptive precautions; and to erase those mistakes abortion will be needed. Second, abortion is so extreme a violation of the Christian code of morality—far more extreme than simple fornication or adultery or homosexuality—that if abortion can be seen as morally justified, then so can all the less extreme forms of sex-related conduct. If you think abortion is permissible, then why shouldn't you think that fornication, etc. are also permissible? And if you're willing to commit abortion, why would you hesitate, except for reasons of personal prudence or taste,[102] to commit adultery and the rest?

It follows from this that it is not enough for you Catholic bishops to go on record as being opposed to abortion. You must also avoid giving the least impression of being "soft" on abortion. But this is precisely the impression you give when, for instance, you hesitate to take strong action against pro-abortion Catholic politicians. And this is the impression the University of Notre Dame[103] gave in May of 2009 when it gave President Obama—a strongly pro-abortion president—an honorary degree and invited him to deliver the principal commencement address. By contrast, the bishop of Fort Wayne-South Bend did exactly the right thing when, following the Notre Dame announcement about the Obama degree and speech, the bishop announced that he would refuse to attend the commencement ceremony held at the famous university in his diocese. And so did dozens of other bishops—including the president of the United States Council of Catholic Bishops, Cardinal Francis George of Chicago—do the right thing when they too denounced the Notre Dame invitation to Obama. After the ND commencement, the United States Conference of Catholic Bishops officially commended the Fort Wayne-South Bend bishop for his stand.[104]

(c) Chastity. Secularism has a highly permissive attitude toward sexual conduct. The attitude is not totally permissive, however. It doesn't say, "Anything goes." Instead it says, "*Almost* anything goes." Such conduct, secularists insist, ought to be regulated by considerations of health, prudence, personal taste, nonviolence, and harm to innocent third parties. But once

---

[102] Most secularists and moral liberals would never engage in homosexual conduct. But they'll tell you that this is not because they think homosexual conduct morally objectionable. It's because such conduct, in itself a morally permissible thing, just happens to be something that they have no taste for. It's like eating oysters— nothing morally objectionable in this, but some people just happen not to like it.

[103] My alma mater, by the way. I have a master's degree in philosophy from ND.

[104] This is a very encouraging sign for those of us who have been hoping that you bishops would take a more effective leadership role in defending the faith against its anti-Christianity enemies. If you bishops continue to move in the same direction, perhaps a book like this one won't be needed in a few years.

---

these are attended to, sex is a morally indifferent matter. Thus secularism has no principled objection to fornication, unmarried cohabitation, or homosexuality—or even adultery, provided the adultery is done with the explicit or tacit permission of the "innocent" spouse.[105] From the secularist point of view, chastity is not a virtue; indeed the notion of chastity as a virtue is either incomprehensible or downright laughable. For many years now American Catholicism has for all practical purposes de-emphasized chastity, not by saying that unchastity is permissible, but by maintaining a discreet near-silence on the topic. The attitude of you bishops and your priests seems to be this: "I'm not blind. I know perfectly well that almost all married Catholics practice contraception during their child-bearing years, and that almost all unmarried young Catholics engage in fornication. So let's just be quiet on the topic of chastity. After all, we don't want to antagonize our parishioners." I don't say it will be easy for you bishops and your priests to begin again, after a lapse of many years, to preach a strict sexual morality; on the contrary, it will be very difficult to do this. But if Catholicism wishes to draw bright lines between itself and the anti-Christian world of secularism and moral liberalism, it must re-assert its ancient emphasis on chastity as a virtue, an extremely important virtue.

(d) Homosexuality. Secularism is particularly aggressive in its contention that homosexuality is morally permissible, and that those who disagree are motivated—not by the findings of sociology, psychology, or philosophy, and not by honest religious conviction—but by bigotry; or in those cases in which the disapprovers of homosexuality *are* motivated by honest religious conviction, then the religion which supplies such motivation is itself bigoted. Say the secularists: "If anti-gay people were true Christians (as they pretend to be) and not hypocrites (as they really are), they would, in a spirit of Christian compassion, give their blessing to same-sex relationships." It is always amusing to see secularists give instruction to Christians as to the true nature of

---

[105] Many secularists would go a bit further and contend that adultery is permissible even without spousal permission provided the adultery is effectively kept secret from the spouse and therefore causes no pain to him or her.

Christianity.[106] They are assisted in this amusing enterprise by liberal Christians who, agreeing that the secularist estimate of the morality of homosexuality is correct and the traditional Christian estimate is incorrect, have themselves decreed that "true" Christianity approves of homosexual conduct in certain circumstances; if Jesus were to return to the world today he would be a great supporter of same-sex marriage, and he would encourage men who are "born gay" to engage in homosexual fornication. Again, it won't be easy for Catholics to condemn homosexual conduct in a world in which such condemnations are routinely met with howls of "bigotry" and "homophobia," but if Catholicism wishes to draw a bright line of division between itself and its secularist foes, it has no choice but to re-assert its traditional teaching on this topic: namely, that homosexual conduct is sinful, is a perversion of nature, and is especially abominable in the eyes of God.

4. Pertaining to devotion

(a) **Ritualism.** Since there seems to be a rough correlation between the degree of a religion's ritualism and the degree of its supernaturalism, and since

---

[106] It is doubly amusing to hear secularists who have rarely or never read the Bible quote the NT passage in which Jesus says, "Judge not, that ye be not judged"—as if Jesus meant, "Be tolerant of homosexuality." In the same amusing category fall those secularists who point out that the OT condemns not just homosexuality but the eating of shellfish, and they make what they imagine to be the telling point that if we consider the former to be an "abomination" then we must take the same view of the latter. These secularists are Scripture "scholars" who are completely unaware of the perennial Christian distinction between the ceremonial and the moral laws of the OT. Equally amusing are those secularists who point out that Jesus in the NT never condemned homosexuality, inferring from that non-condemnation that Jesus approved of homosexuality. Of course Jesus never condemned Roman gladiator games or bribes for voters or arson. Did he therefore approve of such things? What's more, Jesus *did* condemn homosexuality, at least by clear implication. He did so when he spoke of Sodom and Gomorrah as deeply sinful places. And he did so when he held indissoluble heterosexual marriage as the only morally tolerable kind of sexual union.

supernaturalism makes for a bright line between secularism and Christianity, Catholicism should reaffirm its tradition of high and frequent ritualism. There has been a trend in the last 40 years or so, ever since American Catholicism became more "Protestantized," to minimize rituals other than the Mass. This trend should be reversed. Sacred rituals should abound. Revive old ones. Invent new ones.

(b) Latin. When in the days of the Roman Empire, Latin was first used in the liturgies of the Roman Church, it was still a vernacular language. It was the language used in ritual, yes, but it was not a ritual language. Centuries ago it lost its vernacular character, yet was retained in the liturgy; thus it became a ritual language (much as the Coptic language of ancient Egypt is today a ritual language among Egyptian Christians, who long ago gave up speaking Coptic and began to speak Arabic instead). The disappearance of Latin from Catholic Masses about 40 or 50 years ago was, then, a lessening of Catholic ritualism. I grant that saying and hearing the Mass in English was in some ways a gain, but in other ways it was a loss. The loss can be repaired by encouraging Catholics to attend Latin as well as English Masses.[107]

(c) "Gloomy superstition." There is a notorious—and usually misunderstood—passage in the Anglican writings of John Henry Newman that is worth keeping in mind. He says that

> . . . it would be a gain to this country [England], were it vastly more superstitious, more bigoted, more gloomy, more fierce in its religion. Not, of course, that I think the tempers of mind herein implied desirable, which would be an evident absurdity; but I think them infinitely more desirable and more promising than a heathen obduracy, and a cold, self-sufficient, self-wise tranquility." ("The Religion of the Day," found in Newman's *Parochial and Plain Sermons*, I, 24; page 205 of the Ignatius Press edition, 1997.)

---

[107] Thanks to Pope Benedict XVI, there is no longer any canonical barrier to the saying of Latin Masses. But more can be done by bishops to encourage them.

What Newman means to say is this: While both superstition and liberalism are vices that deviate from authentic Christian supernaturalism, superstition is less of a deviation than is liberalism; and so, given a choice of vices, we'd be better off choosing the former than the latter. The lesson to be learned from Newman's comment by you bishops should be this—that while superstition is something legitimately to be feared, this fear should not make you afraid of emphasizing the supernaturalistic element in Catholicism. I offer an illustrative story from my personal experience. In the summer of 2012 my wife and I happened to visit the old shrine of St. Anne de Baupré, a few miles north of Quebec City. When I last visited the place, many years ago, abandoned crutches were a conspicuous feature of the shrine—the crutches having been left by persons who believed themselves to have been miraculously cured as a result of their prayers to St. Anne, the mother of the Virgin. But by the summer of 2012 the crutches had vanished; or at least they were very well-hidden, for I looked hard for them without finding them. No doubt they had vanished because the people in charge at St. Anne de Baupré, having a modern mentality (that is, a mentality partially infected by secularism), have concluded that the old belief in St. Anne-produced miracles was a superstitious thing. And perhaps it was. But if Catholicism is to draw a bright line between itself and secularism, I suspect it would do better to display the crutches than to hide them away. In other words, it is better—or at least less harmful—to err by leaning in the superstitious direction than in the secularist direction.

(d) A prolife ritual. Since abortion is one of the two greatest bones of contention (homosexuality and same-sex marriage being the other) between Catholicism and moral liberalism, the Church would do well to develop rituals having to do with abortion; that is, having to do with the rejection of abortion and the affirmation of the human life of the unborn child. A ceremony might be developed that would involve expectant mothers and their unborn babies: a rite that would take place, let's say, two or three months into the pregnancy, sometime around the point in pregnancy when abortions commonly take place. The ceremony, which would involve prayers for the health and safety of both mother and baby, would have the effect of affirming the humanity of the unborn child while at the same time implicitly declaring the mother's decision to reject the abortion option. This would be, so to speak, a "sacrament of choice." At the very moment that some women, persuaded or seduced by the tenets of secularist moral liberalism, are choosing to abort the "thing" they carry (the tenets of moral liberalism prohibit them from calling this entity a "baby"), Catholic women will be choosing life for their unborn babies.

5. Pertaining to Church Polity

From the time of the Reformation in the 16th century, one of the great differences between Catholicism and Protestantism has had to do with the right of "private judgment" in religion. According to Catholicism the ultimate authority in religion is the hierarchy of the Church, that is, popes and bishops, for it is members of the hierarchy who tell us what is contained in the deposit of Divine Revelation (the Bible plus Sacred Tradition). For Protestantism, by contrast, the final authority in religion was the Bible alone; and since there was nobody—neither pope nor bishop nor anybody else—with the authoritative right to tell us how to interpret the Bible, we individuals would have to rely on our own private judgments. Over the centuries the Protestant belief in the right of private judgment has spread from Bible-reading to many other things. We moderns believe we have the right to "think for ourselves" with regard, not just to the Bible, but to religious questions generally and also to questions of morality, politics, law, economics, art, taste, psychology, sociology, and even (at least so some people believe) medicine. Apart from mathematics and the "hard" sciences,[108] we moderns recognize no authoritative teachers.

In a world in which, outside of math and science, there are no authoritative teachers, the Catholic Church draws a very bright line indeed between itself and its secularist enemies when it asserts that it has the right to teach religious truth authoritatively. For a secularist, hardly anything could be more absurd

---

[108] Perhaps biology doesn't qualify as a "hard" science, but surely it comes close to that. Yet there are those—certain religious conservatives—who reject the authority of professional biologists when it comes to the theory of evolution.

than the idea that there is in the world a body of men, the pope and his bishops, who can teach religious truth with authority. The secularist can understand that once upon a time, many centuries ago, pre-modern people *believed* that there were such religious teaching authorities. But how can anybody, except of course for persons who are deeply ignorant and superstitious, believe such a thing today? When present-day Catholics who are apparently modern and educated and non-superstitious step forward and say, "We still believe that the popes and bishops are custodians and teachers of religious truth; we believe that Jesus left an infallible teaching authority behind when he departed the earth," a truly bright line will have been drawn between Catholicism and secularism.

[end of chapter]

CHAPTER 9

Persuasion Difficulties

In the preceding chapter we have seen that you bishops, if you are to save the Catholic Church in the United States, must draw a very bright line between Catholicism and its great contemporary enemy, anti-Christian secularism (including its ethical subdivision, moral liberalism); and that in doing this you must put a very heavy stress on distinctively Catholic ideas in the realms of knowledge, metaphysics, ethics, devotion, and hierarchical authority. But how is this actually to be accomplished? You cannot of course do it all by yourselves. You need the co-operation of priests, of other religious, and of the laity. How are you to win this co-operation? In other words, when you lead, how can you get your followers to follow? In this chapter I'll make a few suggestions. But they are nothing more than that—mere suggestions. In actual practice, if you bishops are once again to become effective leaders of your flocks, you will have to discover how to do this on an experimental basis, a trial-and-error basis.

Persuading your priests.

First of all, you have to get your diocesan priests on board. In theory the parish priest is the bishop's surrogate. If by some great miracle the bishop could be simultaneously present in each parish in his diocese and had enough time and energy to say all the needed masses, preach all the needed homilies, hear all the needed confessions, do all the needed baptisms, etc., there would be no need for parish priests. But since miracles like this don't happen and never will happen, a bishop needs parish-priest-helpers to carry out his episcopal mission. If you bishops decide you want to save American Catholicism by means of drawing a bright line between your religion and the secularist enemy, you will need full support and assistance from your diocesan priests. Among other things, they will have to give homilies that deal with fornication, abortion, homosexuality, same-sex marriage, physician-assisted suicide, and so on. At election time they will need to give sermons which, usually without mentioning names, remind parishioners that they have a Christian duty, not to mention a citizenship duty, to avoid voting for candidates who are the enemies of Catholicism and its moral teachings. And your priests may even have to tell parishioners that the Democratic Party has been taken over by atheists and anti-Christians. Your problem, dear bishops, is that many of your priests, perhaps even the great majority, don't like to do things like this. They prefer giving homilies addressed to the lukewarm, homilies that tend to confirm their parishioners in their relatively decent and harmless lukewarmness. Such sermons aren't specifically Catholic sermons; instead they are sermons appropriate to a religion that I have called earlier in the book by the name of Generic Christianity. By this, to repeat, I mean a religion that has silently dropped the distinctively Catholic elements of Christian belief and practice, and has been left with a minimal set of beliefs, usually a three-article creed:

- God loves us.[109]
- Jesus was a fine man[110] whom we should take for our ethical model.

---

[109] To this first article is sometimes added the words, "just the way we are." In other words, God, like many a fine psychotherapist, is nonjudgmental. He is a Nice Fellow who has no real objection to our sins.

[110] In Generic Christianity the divinity of Christ is never explicitly denied, but it is rarely stressed.

- We should love[111] our neighbors.

How will you bishops persuade priests who have this Generic Christianity mentality to denounce from the pulpit, for example, abortion and same-sex marriage? It won't be easy.

It will be even less easy given the relative shortage of priests in the United States today. For if you say to a parish priest, "I want you to preach about abortion and homosexuality," and he refuses to do this, what can you do? In the old days a bishop could say in effect, "If you defy me, you'll never make pastor. Worse still, I'll assign you to a parish in the slums or in the boondocks where you'll serve under a grumpy (and perhaps alcoholic) old pastor." You bishops can't do this anymore. Most parishes have only one priest; and so almost every diocesan priest becomes a pastor early in his career. Another factor that makes your episcopal work difficult is the seminary training that your older priests (and of course most of your priests are pretty old guys by now) were receiving in the 1960s and '70s: a training that was more concerned with appreciating the merits of the secularist and semi-secularist critique of Catholicism and its orthodoxy than with stressing the merits of orthodoxy and the shortcomings of secularism and semi-secularism (by which I mean liberal Christianity). This is not to mention the presence in many of those seminaries of ideas and attitudes of sexual permissiveness (often homosexual permissiveness). No doubt many of these deficiencies have been diminished in recent times, but there are still many active priests whose Catholic orthodoxy was "softened" during their seminary years.

Before you can convert your lay people to the idea that their religion is threatened by the prevalence of secularism in American society and culture, you will have to convert your priests. This will not be the work of a summer's day. You will have to instruct them patiently ("in-service training," I suppose it can be called), and you will have to make a strong appeal to the loyalty a

---

[111] One of the prominent aspects of this "love" of neighbor is tolerance, including tolerance of behavior that Catholicism has always counted sinful. Another aspect is that we should promote a strictly material and temporal kind of "social justice," especially by voting for candidates who are politically liberal, usually Democrats.

priest should have to his bishop. And with more than a few you'll have to rely on good old-fashioned brow-beating.

Direct appeals to the laity

In communicating with the lay persons of your diocese, you won't be able to rely totally on the parochial clergy, since, as just noted, many of them aren't all that reliable when it comes to the battle against secularism. Besides, getting the bishop's message to the laity via the parochial clergy is more than a bit old-fashioned. It is medieval, or even pre-medieval; that is, it comes from a day when we did not have modern means of communications. Today, thanks to up-to-date methods of communication, you can appeal "over the heads" of your parish priests to the laity themselves.

How can you do this? To begin with, you can use the diocesan newspapers (of which you are probably the publisher). But this won't get you very far, since such newspapers are generally not very interesting, hence not widely read. Besides, the Catholics who *do* read them are very earnest Catholics, the ones who least need persuading that Catholicism is endangered by secularism. I don't mean that you should *not* use your own newspapers. By all means, *do* use them; but don't expect them to be very effective at persuading the unpersuaded. Your newspapers can, however, be at least a little bit effective at mobilizing those Catholics who are already persuaded. If you want those among your laity who are strongly committed Catholics to phone their state legislators, to turn up at a rally or a prayer meeting, etc., the diocesan newspaper, despite its old-fashionedness, can often be useful.

But if you want to communicate with lay Catholics other than those who are highly committed, you will have to utilize organs of communication that you don't control, in particular local secular newspapers. Average lay Catholics are far more likely to read and pay attention to something written in the secular media than the same thing written in the diocesan paper. But how can you utilize these papers? Let me suggest three ways. (1) For one, you can write an occasional op-ed piece. Your diocese probably has a dozen or more regularly published papers; there is perhaps one metropolitan daily, along with many local dailies and weeklies. The lesser papers are usually hungry for well-written (and even not very well-written) material authored by unpaid outsiders; they will print almost anything a Catholic bishop sends them. And the metropolitan daily, though it prides itself on being more selective, will rarely turn down a well-written piece from the local Catholic bishop. (2) But you don't have to limit yourself to op-ed pieces. The papers probably have one or two local political columnists. These columnists will often, perhaps even usually, be sympathetic to moral values that contradict Catholic values— in other words, they'll be men and women who are themselves secularists or semi-secularists; which means they will be moral liberals, ideological sympathizers with assisted suicide, abortion, homosexuality, same-sex marriage, and sexual permissiveness generally. Nonetheless you should strike up a personal relationship with them; talk with them; discuss issues with them. You won't convince them, of course, and when they choose to report your views they'll usually make it plain that they think you're wrong. But they'll make a more or less honest attempt to understand your views, and they will in all likelihood let the locals know what your views are. (3) Further, you can get into the newspapers by doing something newsworthy, e.g., by forbidding communion to, or even excommunicating, a notoriously pro-choice Catholic politician,[112] or by censuring the local Catholic college because it has extended recognition to an LGBT organization as a legitimate college club. It is relatively easy for a Catholic bishop to make news—just be sure that you do so in a way that educates the laity of your diocese regarding the ongoing struggle between secularism and Catholicism. (4) And of course you can always call a press conference and be confident that it will get good local coverage.

---

[112] I am not necessarily saying that the bishop should sanction these politicians in these ways. Perhaps he should, perhaps he shouldn't. It depends on the politician and the diocese and the circumstances of the moment. At all events, whether or not to do so is a prudential decision, and not an easy one to make. But one thing you can be sure of: if you do impose a drastic sanction on a "dissident" Catholic politician, your action will be big news in local papers and on local TV.

Don't adopt the attitude of wishing for only "favorable" press coverage, for if you do wish for this you'll be wishing for what, in present-day America, is almost impossible. Most of the press won't give you favorable coverage when you talk about, say, sexual conduct, abortion, or same-sex marriage. But they *will* give you coverage. That's all you need. Such coverage of your unfashionable views (that is, your Catholic views) will irritate secularists and Christians of the liberal persuasion; they'll say: "How ridiculous this bishop is! How foolish his medieval mindset!" And they will write letters to the editor telling the world how "out of touch," how "behind the times," how "insensitive," how "lacking in compassion," and how "hypocritical" you are. In other words, by publicly defending the faith against its secularist and semi-secularist enemies, you will provoke local anti-Catholics to come out of the woodwork. But your Catholic flock (i.e., your flock of orthodox or near-orthodox Catholics) will read the coverage too, and they'll say: "How interesting! The bishop seems to be really serious when he says he believes that fornication, unmarried cohabitation, abortion, homosexuality, etc. are sinful. These are not simply pro forma positions that he takes because Rome has told him he has to."

What I've said about newspapers applies also *mutatis mutandis* to radio and TV. Don't be reluctant to be a conspicuous public figure in the secular media. "But," it will be objected, "bishops often don't look good when appearing in the secular media." True enough, but often that's because they try to tone down their Catholicism for the occasion, smooth out its rough edges, so as not to give offense to outsiders. Don't worry about that. Be as Catholic as you possibly can, rough edges and all. When you call a press conference to denounce a legislative bill that would legalize same-sex marriage, don't hesitate to denounce heterosexual cohabitation as well. Keep in mind that when you appear in the secular media the audience you are aiming at is not so much the world in general as it is your Catholic flock. You are not trying to convert the "world" to Catholicism; you're trying to convert Catholics to Catholicism. And if you give offense to outsiders, especially secularist outsiders, that's well and good; you are, after all, trying to draw a bright line between us and them. No matter how you present yourself, secularists will consider you and your beliefs ridiculous; so why bother "softening" your Catholicism? If you don't look and sound good on TV, hire a coach who will teach you the tricks of making a good TV appearance. And if you don't look good because you're overweight,[113] go on a diet. A certain amount of asceticism with regard to food and drink is surely not too much to ask of a bishop who has the Christ-given responsibility of spreading and defending the Gospel.

And don't forget the Internet. The possibilities here are great, especially when it comes to communicating with those of the younger generation. You should have, to begin with, a diocesan website at which you post all your statements on religious, moral, political, and cultural issues. But this, like the diocesan newspaper, is something whose readership/viewership will be limited to those who are already strongly committed Catholics. You also need a website that will draw the attention of less committed *young* Catholics—and this means it will have to be clever and amusing, since young people won't waste their time on websites they find boring. But since bishops have never been especially "clever and amusing" (even though many Catholics, when in the presence of a bishop, pretend that they find him clever and amusing, and this polite pretense sometimes misleads bishops into the delusion that they *are* clever and amusing), this is something you should not try yourselves. If you're lucky enough to stumble across a group of brilliant young Catholics who are operating an anti-secularist website, encourage them; and this encouragement should include a financial subsidy. "How," you may ask, "can a serious business like the 'war' between secularism and Catholicism possibly be amusing?" The answer is, good satire is always amusing; and the ideas of secularism—especially some of its ideas regarding morality—provide rich targets for satire. It is easy to imagine a website with a title like "What are they up to now?" or "Here they go again." I repeat, however: Don't try this yourself; wait till it turns up, then cheer it on. And if it doesn't turn up spontaneously, try to foster it.

---

[113] In a religion that has always laid a heavy stress on asceticism, a well-fed priest is something of a scandal, and a well-fed bishop a considerable scandal.

One more thing. Politicians rely heavily on direct mail. So should you. From time to time send a letter to all the Catholics in your diocese, reminding them, say, that abortion is a great crime, or that same-sex marriage (or its "civil union" equivalent) is a danger to the institution of the married two-parent family; or cautioning them that it is morally indefensible to vote for political candidates who support moral options condemned by Catholicism. And often this "letter" should be an easy-to-read oversized postcard; for persons who are inclined to quickly toss out "junk mail" (that includes almost everybody) can toss out a letter without opening the envelope, but when tossing out a postcard they cannot help but glancing at it and absorbing something of its message.

And of course you can do the same thing by email. Every bishop should collect as many email addresses as possible of the Catholics in his diocese. This is easy to do. Every so often at Sunday Mass—especially masses at Christmas and Easter—ask those in the congregation to fill out a 3 x 5 card with their name and email address. That many dioceses have not done this is a scandal—a sign that you bishops are technological dinosaurs. Dinosaurs won't win the Culture War. Collectively, acting through the United States Conference of Catholic Bishops, you should have a nation-wide network of email addresses. Ideally you'd have the email address of all American Catholics, so that you could communicate with them directly and instantaneously. It is shocking that you don't have such a network. To repeat, dinosaurs won't win the Culture War.

Speaking of the USCCB, it would be very helpful for American bishops acting collectively through the USCCB to issue a pastoral letter on secularism and its "war" against traditional Christianity, a letter that would analyze the cultural-political attack against Catholicism in America and warn "the people of God" about it. This letter would have to talk about many things I have talked about in this book—

- fornication and unmarried cohabitation
- abortion
- homosexuality and same-sex marriage
- atheism and agnosticism
- liberal Christianity (including liberal Catholicism)

- mainline Protestantism
- the mainstream media
- the entertainment industry
- the Democratic Party
- and many other things

Such a letter would have to be long-considered and carefully written. But no matter how carefully written, it will of course be denounced by the enemies of Catholicism, both the external enemies (secularists and liberal Protestants) and the internal enemies (liberal Catholics). You bishops will be called paranoid. You will be told that you are imagining things. You will be reminded that it is absurd—almost insane—to say that a kind of religious persecution is going on in the United States, a land of tremendous religious freedom. If you are not willing to bear these many insults, then don't issue a pastoral letter. But if you are unwilling to expose yourself to attack by the weapons the secularist enemy wields so well, I mean the weapons of ridicule and denunciation, then you might ask yourselves if you are worthy successors of ancient bishops who were willing to face lions or burning at the stake. It is hard to suffer what may be called the "soft martyrdom" of denunciation and ridicule, but it is easier than suffering the real thing, as many of your predecessors have done over the centuries. If you are willing to face actual martyrdom—and I suppose every one of you is, at least in abstract theory, willing to be martyred if need be—then you should be able face the metaphorical martyrdom of public ridicule and denunciation that will be hurled at you by secularists and semi-secularist Catholics.

Catholic colleges and universities

Almost certainly you have a Catholic institution of higher education (or two or three or more of them) in your diocese. In recent decades, many of these "Catholic" institutions have not been especially Catholic; they have tended to follow the path that was earlier followed by America's Protestant colleges and universities, a path leading gradually to the secularization and de-Christianization of these institutions.[114] You bishops have the power to insist that a college remain faithful to its professed Catholicism. For if it doesn't, you can publicly condemn it for its abandonment of Catholicism; and this public condemnation will be widely publicized, probably nationally publicized; and this bad publicity is something the college cannot afford, since it will negatively impact its fund-raising and student recruitment. Or to put this in cruder terms, you can "blackmail" the college into fidelity by threatening public denunciation. Of course, a college's retreat from Catholicism will rarely be so dramatic and clearcut that you'll be justified in applying a clearcut and dramatic denunciation to it. You'll have to engage in a series of partial denunciations. For example, you might criticize a theologian on the faculty for writing a book or article that contradicts Catholic orthodoxy; or you might find fault with the president of the college for permitting an on-campus performance of "The Vagina Monologues"—a theatrical work that emanates from the leftwing of the feminist movement (and leftwing feminism, one must remember, is anti-Christianity feminism), celebrating, under the guise of being pro-woman, unchastity and lesbianism; or you might quarrel with the college's decision to provide facilities for an event co-sponsored by Planned Parenthood; or you might refuse to attend a commencement ceremony at which a pro-choice politician, especially a pro-choice Catholic politician, will be awarded an honorary degree; and so on. Every time you do this, you will in effect be hinting that you have doubts as to the truly Catholic character of this college. It will be an ongoing struggle between you and the college authorities, but in most cases, if you are persistent, the colleges will decide that it's unwise to antagonize you; for public doubts about their Catholic character will give offense to Catholic parents of prospective students and to gift-giving alumni. In other words, most Catholic colleges, faced with the credible threat of episcopal sanctions or denunciations, will dial back on their process of gradual de-Catholicization. But until now most of you bishops have

---

[114] For an excellent historical account of the de-Christianization of the older Protestant colleges, see George Marsden's splendid book, *The Soul of the University*.

done little or nothing along this line. You have allowed the de-Catholicizers at our colleges get away with a little of this and a little of that, until today the Catholicism of many of our "Catholic" institutions of higher education is at best a very watered-down Catholicism, at worst a Catholicism in name only.

Further, you should cultivate personal relations at your Catholic colleges and universities—relations not just with the president and other high-ranking administrators, but also with members of the board of trustees and, last but far from least, with earnest Catholics on the faculty. Very few faculty members at Catholic institutions of higher education are truly earnest about their Catholicism; they are outnumbered on the faculty, usually badly outnumbered, by non-Catholics and lukewarm Catholics. This minority of earnest Catholic professors could use your encouragement as they try to defend the faith on campus.

In the Culture War between Christianity and secularism, Catholic colleges and universities can play—and *should* play—an important role. It is above all in these institutions of higher education that the Church should be doing its *thinking*. Among well-educated Americans today, it is secularism, not Christianity, that has great intellectual prestige. Think of the chief divisions of contemporary American Christianity. (1) Pentecostalism has no intellectual prestige at all. (2) Evangelical Protestantism has only very slight intellectual prestige. This is partly, but only partly, due to its tendency to be skeptical about the theory of biological evolution. "How can we take seriously," it is often asked by the world outside of Evangelicalism, "*any* of the ideas of people who are so anti-intellectual as to reject the fundamental theory of modern biological science?" The low prestige is also due to the fact that conspicuous spokespersons for Evangelicalism, though often very intelligent in a narrow Bible-centered way, rarely seem to be men or woman of broad intellectual culture. (3) Liberal or progressive or modernist Christianity has considerable intellectual prestige. But this is a borrowed prestige, borrowed from secularism. For the typical liberal Christian is either a semi-secularist or an outright secularist pretending to be a Christian. Almost all his ideas and values are the values and ideas of secularism—except that the liberal Christian has sprinkled secularist ideas and values with a perfume of Christian sentimentality. (4) The intellectual prestige of Catholicism ranks higher than that of Pentecostalism and Evangelicalism, to be sure, but in America today not a great deal higher. One rarely hears the expression "Catholic intellectual" used; and on those rare occasions when it is used, it more often refers to an intellectual who just happens to be a Catholic than it does to a person whose intellectualism is a specifically Catholic intellectualism, that is, an intellectualism inspired by the Catholic tradition of ideas.[115] This is a great pity, since Catholicism has an extraordinarily long and rich intellectual tradition.

It is a pity for American Catholicism that Catholic colleges and universities have done a poor job of preserving and appropriating that tradition, for it leaves the Catholic Church in the United States at a great competitive disadvantage in the marketplace of ideas. What's more, it is a pity for American culture as a whole that this Catholic tradition of thought is not contributing to the pluralistic mix that makes up American thought, for it leaves American thought to be blown about by whatever wind of doctrine that happens to be fashionable at the moment. Our national ship of mind[116] increasingly lacks the ballast of a strong tradition. Catholicism is the natural custodian, so to speak, not just of the many centuries of Catholic thought proper (e.g., Augustine, Anselm, Aquinas, Dante, Pascal, Newman, Maritain), but of the classical thought of the ancient world. In the course of its journey through the centuries, Catholicism adopted and made its own Plato, Aristotle, Cicero, Virgil, etc. In failing to appropriate its own tradition, then, Catholic higher education has also failed to appropriate the classical tradition of the Western World; and having failed to do so, it cannot deliver this tradition to American society at large. And if Catholicism, its natural guardian, can't deliver it, then it just

---

[115] For clarity's sake, let me give three examples of a contemporary Catholic intellectual, i.e., an intellectual whose intellectualism is of Catholic inspiration: Pope Benedict XVI, the late Fr. Stanley Jaki, Professor Robert George of Princeton, and Garry Wills. Some readers will object to the inclusion of Wills on this list, since they consider his Catholic orthodoxy and loyalty dubious, to say the least. But even if you take the most negative view of Wills, you will still have to concede that his mind is a mind shaped by Catholic ideas and themes.

[116] On the analogy of "ship of state."

won't be delivered, for there is nobody else who *can* deliver it. Once upon a time American Protestantism was also steeped in classical learning, but this ended about a century ago as Protestantism divided into a modernist wing and a fundamentalist wing. Modernists, who were completely preoccupied with ideas that were fashionable and up-to-date, ceased being concerned with classical learning and ancient ideas; while fundamentalists turned in the direction of religion based on feeling, on a "decision for Christ," and on a profoundly anti-intellectual biblical literalism.

Up until the 1960s American Catholic colleges were very Catholic, but, with only a few exceptions, they weren't very intellectual. Their faculties were almost 100 percent Catholic, and a clear majority of the professors were priests (in men's colleges) or nuns (in women's colleges). These colleges required that students take a heavy load of Thomistic philosophy and theology courses, but this was a "textbook Thomism" that did little to stimulate the intellectual life of students. Besides, the students usually came from a social class background that did little to prepare them for the life of mind and high culture. Typically they were from blue-collar families, the children or grandchildren of immigrants from Ireland, Italy, Germany, Quebec, and the Slavic countries. They did not attend college to develop the life of mind; they attended so they could get better jobs than their parents and climb a few rungs upward on the socio-economic ladder. And those who came from a somewhat higher socio-economic background (the "lace-curtain Irish," for example) were not much better prepared to develop the life of mind, for they and their families belonged to a Catholic subculture that was intellectually narrow-minded: strongly attached to Catholicism but relatively incurious about—and often afraid of—the world of ideas and values that flourished outside the Catholic "ghetto."

But then in the 1960s and '70s everything changed in Catholic higher education, as it did during those decades in so much else in American life. Catholic colleges decided to upgrade their academic quality. This upgrading had two aspects. (1) Priests and nuns came to make up a smaller and smaller percentage of Catholic college faculties. In the heyday of priest- and nun-dominated Catholic colleges, being a priest or nun would get you a professorship even if your academic abilities and achievements were not very great. Of course you had to have some minimum qualification, but as long as you had that, you would get appointed or promoted. Why? Two reasons. First, because it was a way of assuring that the college continued to have a genuinely Catholic character. Second, it was *cheap*. Priests and nuns had taken vows of poverty, so the college could retain their services by paying for their room and board and not much more. It was a way of keeping tuition fees low—an important consideration when colleges were educating boys and girls with blue-collar parents.[117] The decline in faculty priests and nuns, however, was not mainly the result of a decision to have fewer priests and nuns. For the most part it was a function of the new fact that in the '60s and '70s religious vocations were in decline. There were fewer priests and nuns available: many were leaving the priesthood and the convent, and very few new recruits were coming in. (2) Catholic colleges began hiring teachers, and to a lesser extent administrators, on the basis of their academic qualifications, regardless of religious affiliation or clerical status. If you were a Protestant or a Jew or an agnostic or an atheist, and you had a doctoral degree from a first-rate university, you had an excellent chance of getting hired at a Catholic institution of higher education.

As a result of these two changes, Catholic colleges became academically far better than they had ever been—and at the same time they became far less Catholic than they had ever been. Since it is the custom in American higher education that the faculty of academic department X have a very strong voice, maybe even an absolute voice, in hiring and promoting and granting tenure to teachers in department X, it is far from easy to re-Catholicize a Catholic college faculty once in has been, for all practical purposes, de-Catholicized. As a result of all this, many once-Catholic colleges are today barely Catholic. One of the signs of this is the fact that students in today's Catholic colleges no longer have the heavy requirements in philosophy and theology that their

---

[117] When I entered Providence College as a freshman in the fall of 1956, tuition was $400 per year. It was predominantly a commuter college in those days, with only a small number of residential students. Today it is primarily a residential college, and tuition is $42,385 per year.

predecessor had decades ago. What's more, theology has been replaced with something called "religious studies."

As bishops, you should give strong support to those colleges in your diocese that have remained genuinely Catholic, you should encourage the re-Catholicization of those that have drifted away from Catholicism, and you should publicly denounce as un-Catholic those "Catholic" colleges that have drifted so far from Catholicism that they have become Catholic in name only (CINO).

Dealing with Catholic politicians

In the Culture War between Christianity and secularism[118] one of the chief battlefields, as everybody knows, is the great and never-quiet battlefield of politics and government. Those on both the Christian and the secularist sides in this war use politics, politicians, and political parties to advance their agendas (although in my opinion the secularist side uses these things with more skill and greater effect). To consider only the two most conspicuous issues, abortion and homosexuality, the secularist movement has for many years persuaded and pressured politicians (usually Democrats) to do, among other things, the following:

- nominate, when a Democrat occupies the White House, justices to the US Supreme Court who will preserve a constitutional right to abortion and who will "discover" a constitutional right to same-sex marriage
- block the appointment, when a Republican is in the White House, of US Supreme Court justices who might overturn *Roe v. Wade*
- provide government funds for Planned Parenthood and other abortion-providing and abortion-promoting agencies

---

[118] I should note that the struggle between Christianity and secularism is only one part of the Culture War. Other parts have to do with taxation, size of government, illegal immigration, gun control, and military affairs. In this book, however, I am concerned only with Christianity vs. secularism aspect of the Culture War.

- pay for Medicaid abortions
- include coverage for abortion in the national health-care plan
- legalize same-sex marriage
- repeal the federal Defense of Marriage Act (DOMA)
- permit persons who are openly gay or lesbian (or bisexual) to serve in the military
- instruct public school children that opposition to homosexuality (or bisexuality or transgenderism) springs from bigotry and hatred; that it is a prejudice akin to racism

On the other side of the Culture War, conservative Christians (usually this means Evangelical Protestants, less often it means orthodox Catholics) pressure and persuade politicians (almost always Republicans) to do exactly the opposite.

The Culture War between Christianity and secularism is of course being fought on other battlefields as well, not just in politics; but there is no question that politics is one of its more important fields of struggle. Every time secularists prevail in one of these political struggles, and they prevail fairly often, American culture gets just a bit more de-Christianized, gets to provide a more toxic cultural atmosphere in which Catholic parents will have to raise children. If things don't change, this cultural atmosphere will soon be so un-Christian that Catholic parents will have to place their children on moral and religious respirators. Because of the cultural importance of the political struggle, you bishops cannot absent yourselves from it. If you do everything else right, yet keep out of politics, this will be like boxing with one hand tied behind your back.

But your involvement in politics cannot be—*must* not be—a partisan involvement. In the Culture War political struggles the Democratic Party usually has sided with the anti-Christian secularists (as I pointed out above in chapter seven) while the Republican Party has usually sided with the Christians. This has led many Catholic laypersons, including many of the most loyal and orthodox Catholics, not just to vote Republican but to conclude that the Republican Party is America's Christian party: God's party. Accordingly they'd like to see the bishops throw their support behind the Republicans.

Were you to do this, you would of course be making a gigantic mistake—as you realize; which explains why you have generally not done this. Not one of you, thank heaven, has announced that the letters GOP stand for "God's Own Party." During the last two hundred years or so, the Catholic Church in Europe has had a long and very sad history of supporting pro-Catholic political parties in France, Spain, Italy, and Germany; and your reluctance to endorse the Republican Party is the result, I presume, not just of your timidity (which you seem to be amply supplied with), but of your having learned the lessons of this sad history. The trouble with the Church's allowing itself to get tied closely to a political party is threefold. (1) This pro-Catholic party, no matter how pure it may be at the outset of its alliance with the Church, will eventually become impure; and if it comes to power (and maybe even if it does not), it is almost inevitable—as a result of human nature or at least as the result of the nature of political animals—that it will be marked by minor and major corruption. An alliance with a dirty party will make the Church dirty ("If you lie down with dogs you'll get fleas"). (2) No matter how dedicated the party may be to issues the Church is concerned with (e.g., abortion and same-sex marriage), it will also have to take stands on a multitude of other issues (e.g., taxes, education, national defense, transportation, energy, immigration, health care, housing, welfare payments). As a result of its association with the party, the Church will be perceived as endorsing the party's entire agenda, and this endorsement will antagonize opponents of this or that item on the party's agenda, thus needlessly multiplying the number of enemies the Church has. (3) The party, for any number of reasons, may go into decline and suffer a long period of eclipse[119] or even complete collapse; and in such a case it is probable that the Church,

---

[119] By a political "eclipse" I mean a lengthy period during which a party declines from a dominant to a very secondary position in a nation's political life. The Democratic Party, because it had taken the "wrong" position on slavery and secession, suffered an eclipse that lasted from the election of Lincoln (1860) till the first election of Franklin Roosevelt (1932). And the Republican Party, because it took the "wrong" position on dealing with the Great Depression, suffered an eclipse that lasted from the coming of FDR (1932) till the victories of Ronald Reagan (1980) and Newt Gingrich (1994).

having become in large measure a political thing, will suffer a corresponding eclipse or collapse.

There are, however, *nonpartisan* ways of affecting the political process. You must concentrate on issues and personalities, not parties. Above all you must concentrate on those issues that are essential to the survival of Catholicism, e.g., abortion and same-sex marriage—issues that are being used by the enemies of Catholicism (and traditional Protestantism) to destroy the religion. You can also involve yourselves, if you like, on issues like capital punishment and help for the poor. But these, when measured in terms of the health and survival of Catholicism, are less important issues; for your secularist opponents are not using these issues to undermine and destroy Christianity, which is the way they *are* using the issues of abortion and same-sex marriage; indeed on issues like poverty and the death penalty you often find that you and many secularists are on the same side.

But how can you do this? How can you be politically influential without being partisan? The first thing you should do, I suggest, is give up your style of issuing *abstract* condemnations of Catholic politicians who are supportive of, say, abortion rights; or at least supplement these abstractions and give them flesh, blood, muscles, and bones by *naming names*. You cannot content yourselves with saying that "Catholic elected officials" (a ghostly category) must not do so and so. In the real world of American politics, such abstractions mean little or nothing. They don't register with voters, they are very uninteresting to the press, and they slide off their intended political targets like water from a duck's back. When Catholic prochoice politicians happen to be confronted by the press or the public with these abstract episcopal denunciations, they have learned either to ignore them or simply to reply, "I have the greatest respect in the world for the bishops of my Church, especially my own bishop, and I agree with most of their opinions, especially those relating to poverty and immigration and world peace, but in this particular case we happen not see eye to eye. I have to represent *all* my constituents, not just Catholics. Besides, many of my Catholic constituents don't agree with the bishop on reproductive rights or marriage equality"—and they find that such a reply usually puts the matter to rest. If you bishops want to have any kind of serious impact you have to denounce not abstractions but concrete individuals who have real names and real faces and real addresses and real telephone numbers. Only then will the press and the public sit up and take notice; only then will politicians have a hard time slipping past your attack.

But how do you denounce them by name? Well, you could have all the pastors in your diocese read a letter from you to their parishioners at a weekend Mass; or you could call a press conference; or you could send an email or a letter (or oversized postcard) to all the Catholics in your diocese; or better still, you could do all these things simultaneously. And when you deliver your message in these ways, what precisely will be the content of the message? It could simply be the denunciation itself: "[Name] has supported, and tells me that he intends to persist in his/her support, for abortion—and from a Catholic point of view this is thoroughly unacceptable." Or you could say the foregoing and add to it words like these: "And therefore I have asked [Name] to abstain from participating in the Eucharist until he/she changes his pro-abortion ways; and I have instructed my priests not to offer communion to him/her until that time." Or you could add something even stronger: "And therefore I have formally excommunicated [Name]. Until he/she repents and abandons his/her pro-abortion ways, he/she is not a member of the Catholic Church." I don't mean to say here which of these messages a bishop ought to deliver; for the decision to take this or that line of action is a prudential decision that depends on circumstances of time, place, and person. All I'm saying is that these options—all of them strong options—are available to a bishop; he has all these arrows, and maybe more, in his quiver.

Of course you, as a bishop, can't very well begin public sanctions or denunciations of Catholic politicians without first giving them fair warning. You should do what I believe many bishops have actually done, namely, meet with them and make an earnest attempt, in your best pastoral manner, to persuade them to vote and act in a way that is consistent with their Catholicism. Next you should threaten them with sanctions and denunciations. Only after these attempts have clearly failed should you proceed to actual sanctions and denunciations. So you needn't rush. On the other hand, your patience should not last forever.

In fairness, it should be added that if the politician promises to behave the way a Catholic politician should behave, you the bishop ought to promise that you will do your level best to see to it that he doesn't pay a heavy price for his fidelity to the teachings of the Church. After all, it's politics we're talking about, politics in a democratic society. In a political society like ours, things have been constitutionally arranged so that politicians will on the whole be responsive to the wishes of the voters. If not, they won't get into office in the first place or, if in, will soon find themselves thrown out. It's hard to blame a Catholic politician who is prochoice when that's the way his Catholic voters want him to be or at least are content that he be. Who can be surprised when a Catholic politician decides that he won't become a political martyr, that he won't do the right thing (from a Catholic point of view) if it means that his political life will be terminated (aborted, as it were) by the voters? You the bishop, in the course of your pastoral counseling of the politician, will have to assure him/her that you will educate your parish priests and laity so that they appreciate the politician's Catholic fidelity and don't hold it against him on Election Day. Is it fair to insist that the politician do the right thing when the parish priests and the men and women in the pews are *not* doing the right thing? Why should the senator, congressman, governor, state legislator, mayor, or city councilor have to be the only Catholics to do the right thing?

Rich Catholics

One last point as to how bishops can influence Catholic politicians. Although the United States is in a real sense a representative democracy (for the people are allowed to vote), this democracy has almost always contained a strong oligarchic component, and today the oligarchic component is greater than ever, and it is conceivable, if current trends continue, that the United States will eventually be more oligarchic than democratic—if it isn't already. You bishops, when you think about politics, should be well aware of this. And you should use this knowledge to your advantage.

Every bishop, I'm sure, has a list of the rich Catholics in his diocese. He calls on these rich Catholics to raise and to give money to the diocese and its good works, e.g., Catholic schools, hospitals, and social welfare agencies. In all probability these rich Catholics, quite apart from their associations with the Church, have many connections with one another—in business, philanthropy, community activities, and so on. Their work in helping the Church strengthens and extends these connections; it allows them to meet and work with big shots like themselves, thereby helping their more secular and temporal interests. And of course many of these rich Catholics also have political interests and a desire for political influence; consequently they contribute money to political candidates, especially candidates for high office; and they often have personal friendships with these politicians, dining with them, inviting them to their vacation houses, taking them for cruises on their boats, etc. Now, it would not be an impossible thing for a bishop to encourage at least some of his rich Catholics to work together and use their political connections and contributions to influence politicians on questions like abortion and same-sex marriage. It would not be easy for a politician, especially one in a state or congressional district having a significant number of rich Catholics, to ignore a co-ordinated effort on the part of these rich men and women to influence the politician's views—or at all events his voting habits—on, say, abortion and same-sex marriage.

The obvious objection to such a suggestion is that a bishop who did this would be violating at least the spirit, if not the actual letter, of "separation of church and state." And could he be violating the letter too, a violation that could get him and his diocese in trouble with the Internal Revenue Service? Perhaps the IRS will decide that the Catholic Church in diocese X is functioning as a political organization and therefore will have to lose its tax-exempt status: contributions to the Catholic Church and its agencies in diocese X will no longer be deductible for the contributors.

The answer to the IRS objection is that the bishop can do what I suggest without running afoul of the IRS. For one thing, the bishop as an individual is a citizen too, just like any other citizen; and as an individual citizen he has a right to try to influence elected officials. Moreover, in attempting to exert this influence he has a right, as does everybody else, to co-ordinate his efforts with the efforts of others (in the case supposed, this co-ordination would be with the efforts of rich Catholics). The important thing here is that the bishop operate not *qua* bishop but *qua* individual American citizen. The typical bishop will have a variety of relationships with his rich Catholics. The spectrum will run from close friendships at one extreme to very impersonal relations at the other. Those at the latter extreme barely know the bishop in a personal way, and in some cases they may even dislike him; but they feel obliged as Catholics to contribute money for the well-being of the diocese and its institutions. When you as a bishop ask your rich Catholics to use their wealth as well as their connections with other wealthy persons to influence the conduct of politicians, it is your close friends you will approach. You will approach them in a friend-to-friend way, with no suggestion that they as lay Catholics are bound to obey you as their ecclesiastical superior. As for the rich Catholics who are virtual strangers to you, you won't approach them at all. They will be approached through the network of connections that runs through a number of intermediate steps from your close friends to the strangers. The bishop will not be the "chairman" of this co-ordinated effort. The effort will be a lay effort, directed by rich friends of the bishop. Your role will simply be to initiate the project and to cheer it on. You will say, in effect, to a few of your carefully chosen rich friends: "Look, it's a great shame that our fellow Catholic Senator A (or Governor B or Congressman C) seems to be in thrall to the prochoice lobby. Can't we do something about it? Can't we use our money—or rather, *your* money, since I myself have very little—to bring A (or B or C) back to the paths of righteousness? You've got a lot of rich friends. Can't you do something about this?"

Further, the bishop's role in all this can be unseen by the public. When the bishop meets for lunch or dinner with a small number of his rich friends, the public doesn't have to know this, neither the Catholic public nor the public in general. Nor does the IRS have to know.

In saying this I don't mean that the bishop can or should conceal some illegal or improper activity. Far from it. I have argued that the activity is perfectly legal and proper. But it is one thing to stay within the limits of IRS rules; it is something else to act in such a way as to invite a public misperception of what's going on. If the bishop, instead of initiating this political effort by meeting quietly with a small group of his rich friends, were to launch the political effort in a public and conspicuous way, it is certain that some anti-Catholic organizations (e.g., Americans United for Separation of Church and State or the American Civil Liberties Union) would let out a great public howl, and it is very probable that they would file complaints with the IRS. Of course the complaints would be dismissed in the end, but in the meantime they could be a major annoyance. Worse still, many Catholics, operating with a crude and incorrect notion of what the principle of separation of church and state means, would be shocked and offended.

I don't mean to suggest that it will be easy to mobilize rich Catholics to influence politicians on matters like abortion and same-sex marriage. It won't be. For one thing, many rich Catholics have little objection to abortion and same-sex marriage. They object to government policies that are bad for business, but abortion and same-sex marriage are not bad for business; or if they are bad for business, they are so in such subtle and virtually undetectable ways that nobody notices. To win the co-operation of wealthy Catholics in an effort to persuade Catholic politicians to be truly Catholic will take more than a few words by the bishop at a single lunch with his friends. What I do mean to suggest is that if a significant portion of the rich Catholics in a diocese were to co-ordinate their political efforts in this manner, the results could be tremendous. Such results would justify the trouble it would be for a bishop and his rich friends to bring them about.

[end of chapter]

CHAPTER 10

One Last Thing

Well, my dear bishops, here we are at the end of this long letter. My apologies if I have hurt anybody's feelings. I have tried to bear in mind the remarks of Thomas Aquinas that I quoted in the opening chapter of this book. I have tried to bear in mind (1) his words authorizing me to criticize you. He said that "the fraternal correction which is an act of charity is within the competency of everyone in respect of any person towards whom he is bound by charity, provided there is something in that person which requires correction." Since, as I think every attentive Catholic knows, and as I have shown in spades in the course of this book, there has been "something" in your order that has required fraternal correction, I have offered that correction in what I hope is a spirit of Christian charity. I have also tried to bear in mind (2) his caution that this correction should be done "in a becoming manner, not with impudence and harshness, but with gentleness and respect." If I have sometimes, in a fit of literary passion, crossed the line and spoken to you with a certain amount of "impudence and harshness," I hope this sin has been no more than venial, and I apologize for any impudence and harshness, while asking your forgiveness.

But the important thing at the moment is not your past mistakes but your future action. Much has been lost, but not everything. You, with the help of God, can still rescue the Catholic Church in the United States, a Church that is sinking fast but has not yet gone under for the third time. If you have intelligence and courage, and if you revivify your own personal commitment to the Catholic religion, you can provide the leadership badly needed by the Catholic people of the United States—and until now *badly* lacking. It will of course be no easy task. Your enemies have powerful positions in the mainstream media, the entertainment industry, America's leading colleges and universities, the Democratic Party, and (when that party controls the White House and the Congress) the very government of the United States of America. Most of all, your enemy will be the now-dominant culture of the United States. Up until the 1960s the dominant American culture had been a more or less liberal Protestant culture: a culture not entirely friendly to Catholicism, but at the same time not entirely unfriendly. But the culture that has become increasingly dominant over the last 40 or 50 years is a thoroughly secular culture—nay, a secularist culture; that is, a culture that is hostile to any kind of supernatural religion, especially Christianity, and above all Catholicism. This secularism is the taken-for-granted worldview and accompanying morality of those who are today culturally dominant in the United States: and by "those who are today culturally dominant" I mean not only the outright secularists (who are atheists or agnostics) but also the semi-secularists who call themselves "liberal" or "progressive" or "modernist" Christians, all of whose "new" ideas and values are borrowed from the outright secularists. If the United States becomes a thoroughly secularized nation, American Catholicism probably won't perish entirely. A hundred years from now you'll still be able to find Catholics in the United States, just as, in Egypt you still find (Coptic) Christians almost 1,400 years after the Arab/Muslim conquest of that country. But Catholicism will be a social insignificant religion, a hole-in-the-corner religion; and this will be true of old-fashioned Protestantism as well. The fight you have to fight, dear bishops, is a fight to enable Catholicism to survive in America as something better than a hole-in-the-corner religion.

Mention of the surviving Christian remnant in Egypt reminds me of an objection I sometimes hear from Catholics when I express my fears about a great decline of Catholicism. They remind me of the words of Jesus to Peter:

"Thou art Peter, and upon this rock I shall build my Church, and the gates of Hell will not prevail against it"—the words that promise that the Church will never perish from the Earth. Fine. But notice that Jesus did not promise that the Church would survive in any particular place. He did not say that the gates of Hell will not pervade against his religion in the United States of America. In the course of centuries the Catholic religion has vanished, or virtually vanished, in many places where it once held sway: in the Mideast, where it was replaced by Islam; in North Africa, again replaced by Islam; and in much of Northern Europe, replaced by various kinds of Protestantism. If it vanished in all these places without invalidating the promise of Jesus to Peter, why can't it vanish in the United States? Today it is gradually fading away in much of Europe and in Canada and the United States, being replaced by secularism; and this doesn't invalidate the promise to Peter, for the Catholic religion survives, and even flourishes, in much of the Third World.

Two factors give me hope that there will be a great revival of Catholicism (and of traditional Protestantism as well) in the United States—for despite my pessimism about the future of American Catholicism, I have not yet given way to utter despair. One of these is the horrors that are being produced, and will be produced in even greater abundance in the future, by the cultural reign of atheistic secularism. For sooner or later these horrors are bound to produce a reaction in the direction of sanity. At the moment these horrors can be seen most clearly in matters associated with sexual conduct, byproducts of the sexual revolution that began in the early to middle 1960s—the killing of millions of unborn babies; the glorification of unnatural sexual relations; a sky-high rate of out-of-wedlock births; the disintegration of the married two-parent family; millions and millions of kids growing up without fathers and without the financial, psychological, and moral support that fathers are supposed to provide, and did routinely provide in the old days before the sexual revolution of the 1960s and '70s; sex among teens who are far too young to be dealing with sex; the spread of sexually transmitted diseases; the immense expansion of the pornography industry; the applause of the absurdity called transgenderism; the growing sympathy for polyamory; even the growing sympathy for pedophilia (except of course when the pedophilia is committed by Catholic priests), etc. These evils and perversions, awful in themselves, lead to further awful consequences, e.g., gangs and crime and violence (up to and including murder) in urban neighborhoods in which fatherlessness abounds. The problems of gangs and crime and violence are most obvious at present in black ghettos and, to a slightly lesser extent, in lower-class Latino barrios. But the social cancer of broken families and fatherlessness is metastasizing, spreading relentlessly to the white non-Latino portion of the American population.

However, the pro-Catholicism and pro-Christianity reaction I'm hoping for, a reaction based on the horrors resulting from atheistic secularism (a reaction that might be called "a revolution arising from revulsion"), will not be produced by the evils of the moral/sexual revolution alone. If the evils of the sexual revolution were alone sufficient to produce the desired reaction, this reaction would already have taken place; for the evils of the sexual revolution are by this late date perfectly evident for anyone who has eyes to see. But there are more evils to come. In the secularist "war" against Christianity, traditional sexual morality is the first domino to fall. Others will almost certainly follow. For Christianity is an integrated whole. Get rid of its sexual morality, and you will undermine the rest of its moral system. Many atheists believe that you can get rid of Christianity and its "out of date" sexual morality while leaving in place its love-your-neighbor mentality. But this is an illusion. Nietzsche knew better. "God is dead," he famously said—meaning that the belief in the God of Christianity is dying out in the Euro-American modern world. And when belief in the God of Christianity vanishes, so will belief in Christian morality; and not just Christian sexual morality but Christian morality altogether—a morality created, as Nietzsche saw it, by the resentment that "weak" persons feel for "strong" persons; hence a morality that exalts such values as pity and sympathy and human brotherhood and human equality. Nietzsche rejoiced at the likelihood of this development. He rejoiced to think that once the world rids itself of the "slave" morality of Christianity (as well as its derivative moralities of democracy and socialism), the way will be open for something like a restoration of the "noble" morality that once flourished in the pre-Socratic ages of ancient Greece—an anti-Christian, anti-democratic, anti-socialist morality of strong and self-reliant persons; an anti-hedonist morality that aims, not at ease and comfort and pleasure, but at a life of challenge and difficulty. Was Nietzsche right in his prediction of what will follow the abolition of Christianity? I don't know. But his example shows that it is far from self-evident that getting rid of Christianity will leave us, as atheists and their semi-atheistic fellow travelers (that is, liberal Christians) like to believe, with a "love your neighbor" morality. Further, leaving Nietzsche the theorist and turning to the world of actual affairs, the two great 20th century experiments at abolishing Christianity—Nazism[120] in Germany, Communism in Russia and elsewhere—give no reason to believe that the abolition of Christianity will leave us with a "love your neighbor" morality.

And it is not just *moral* horrors that are likely to issue from present-day atheism and semi-atheism. It is very probable that there will be *intellectual* horrors as well. Contemporary secularism is characterized by a high degree of skepticism—not just skepticism about religion, philosophy, and morality, but a generalized talent for skepticism; there is almost nothing a diehard secularist is unable to doubt if he puts his mind to it. At bottom the thoroughgoing secularist doubts that reality is intelligible. And who can be surprised at this? For many centuries the world, or at least the Western world, has believed that the universe is the creation of God and that God is rational; thus the universe is intelligible. Take the rational creator away, and what happens to belief in the intelligibility of the universe? It may survive for a while—maybe for a few generations—by force of old habit. But it is unlikely that it will be sustained in the long run. Truth will no longer be defined as a correspondence between the mind and reality. Instead it will be defined as what we all have been persuaded to agree upon, never mind whether this agreement is based on knowledge or a lie; for there will be no difference between agreed-upon knowledge and an agreed-upon lie.

---

[120]   If Nietzsche had lived long enough to see them (and if while living long he had retained his sanity), it is very likely that he would have deplored Hitler and the Nazis. All the same, it is clear that Nietzsche's ideas provided more than a small amount of the ideas of Nazism. The Nazis held that their "hardness" was the kind of post-Christian thing Nietzsche admired.

In any case, I think the day will come when the horrors of atheism and secularism will disgust almost everyone and drive our culture back in the direction of a revival of Christianity in general and of Catholicism in particular—a revolution through revulsion, as I have called it. But when will this be? A hundred years from now? Two hundred? Three? Four?

For those who don't like to wait that long, there is already in the United States an encouraging sign of the revival of Catholicism. I refer to the emergence of a new breed of priests and nuns—priests and nuns who are not full of the so-called "spirit of Vatican II." They may be full of the *genuine* spirit of Vatican II, but not of the very un-Catholic spirit that has been masquerading under that name for almost a half-century now. This new breed I am talking about did not grow up in the pre-1960s era; they did not experience the cultural revolution of the 1960s and '70s as a positive thing which, despite certain imperfections, could be blended with Christianity. No, they came along later. They have seen the effects of the cultural revolution, including the sexual revolution, and they have been horrified. In choosing the religious life, they have not simply made a positive choice *for* Catholicism; they have at the same time made a negative choice *against* secularism and all its works and all its pomps. And in making this negative choice, they have preserved their Catholicism from contamination by its anti-Christian opposite, a contamination that affected the Catholicism of an earlier generation. It is too early to tell if this new breed of priests and nuns will be numerous enough to make a real difference in American Catholicism. A handful won't be enough. Great numbers will be needed. But the appearance of this new breed is very encouraging, the most encouraging fact about American Catholicism in nearly fifty years.

And from the ranks of these new priests will emerge new bishops—indeed new bishops are already emerging; your order, my dear bishops, is improving on an almost monthly basis. If in the decades ahead your ranks contain enough of these "new breed" bishops, your order may redeem its good name, a name that has been to a very great extent disgraced for much of the last half-century. You new bishops may provide American Catholicism with the leadership it requires—a leadership that will once again feed the hungry sheep who for years now have been looking up without being fed. For the Catholic religion to flourish in the United States, everything—well, almost everything—depends on high-quality episcopal leadership. If we are fortunate enough to get this good leadership, perhaps we won't have to wait two or three centuries for a revival of American Catholicism. Who knows?

[end of book]

APPENDIX I

Utilitarianism

One way to understand moral liberalism, I suggest, is to see it as a 20th and 21st century survival of 19th century Utilitarianism.[121] According to the Utilitarian theory, when acting we have a duty to choose that course of behavior that will best promote the happiness of all sentient beings, animals and humans—with "happiness" being defined hedonistically, that is, as pleasure plus freedom from pain. No doubt the pleasures and pains of human beings are the pleasures and pains we most have to take into consideration, not because humans are intrinsically more valuable than the so-called lower animals, but because humans have a far greater capacity for pleasure and pain than have these lower animals. There are however two great weaknesses in Utilitarian theory that make it almost impossible for our contemporaries to hold the theory in its original form; and thus if you wish to be a Utilitarian today you will almost certainly modify the original theory. One of these difficulties is that it is virtually impossible to look into the future and correctly predict which among several possible lines of action will result in the greatest happiness for mankind over the long run. For the "long run" may last hundreds

---

[121] The two classic (though somewhat incompatible) formulations of the Utilitarian theory of morality are Jeremy Bentham's *An Introduction to the Principles of Morals and Legislation* (1789) and John Stuart Mill's *Utilitarianism* (1861).

of years, or even thousands or millions, and who can say what the long-run consequences of today's actions may be? For instance, when Hitler's ancestors, perhaps two Tyrolean peasants, married sometime in the 13th or 14th or15th century, who could foresee that this apparently benign marriage would lead eventually to World War II and the Holocaust? But it did. And so, it now turns out on Utilitarian principles that it was morally wrong of those two peasants to wed. Or was it? For perhaps all the other descendants of that original pair have produced, or will eventually produce, enough happiness in the world to overbalance the misery produced by Hitler in the 20th century. It is obviously absurd, then, for us to count *all* the pleasant and unpleasant consequences of this or that action when we wish to give a moral evaluation of that action; and so, if you want to be a Utilitarian today, you will probably depart from pure Benthamism and count only the *reasonably foreseeable* consequences of today's action. This is more reasonable, to be sure, but it greatly reduces the difference between Utilitarianism and other theories of morality, for moralists of all stripes—as well as legal theorists of all stripes—have always said that we have to take into consideration, not all consequences of our conduct, but only reasonably foreseeable consequences.

A second great difficulty is that Stalin and Hitler used—and others still use today—arguments of the Utilitarian type to justify mass murder and other crimes; that is, they used and still use arguments that say in effect, "A sufficiently good end justifies means that most people would call immoral." I don't mean to say that Bentham and Mill promoted conduct that conflicted with the moral beliefs of ordinary decent people. No, for Mill and Bentham were decent people themselves; they would have been horrified to witness the careers of Hitler and Stalin; and they would have been doubly horrified if they found that these homicidal monsters were justifying their wickedness by arguments of the Utilitarian type. Bentham and Mill wanted radical reform of social, economic, and political institutions, but they were relatively conservative when it came to the rules of personal morality. Their Utilitarianism justified radical political reform while at the same time justifying a great deal (though not all) of the rules of conventional personal morality. Further, Stalin and Hitler did not claim to be disciples of Bentham and Mill; I doubt that there is a single reference to either man in the speeches and writings of the two great totalitarian dictators. But they argued—in the Utilitarian mode—that the consequences of their mass murders would prove in the long run to be beneficial for the human race. Kill the Jews or kill the kulaks, and the world (so the reasoning went) will be a better place, at least in the long run. Of course a Utilitarian can argue that the mass murders of Hitler and Stalin did in fact *not* increase the happiness of the human race; exactly the contrary, they greatly increased our collective misery. And thus these murders cannot be justified on Utilitarian grounds; just the opposite—they have to be condemned. True enough, but the habit of thinking in a Utilitarian way can lead, and has led, to mass murder and other great crimes, even if the murderer happens to make erroneous calculations. What's more, it doesn't take great imagination to think of a scenario in which great violations of (conventional) morality can actually lead to increased happiness for humankind generally.

In any case, if you'd like to be a Utilitarian today, you'll be mindful of the "end-justifies-the-means" danger, and you'll also be mindful of the difficulties involved in trying to make predictions as to how today's behavior will turn out in the long run. Accordingly, while you will still hold that the long-term happiness of the human race (and of other animals) is the correct measure of human morality, you will be relatively cautious when taking positive steps to promote that happiness. You will advance only those schemes whose beneficial consequences one can reasonably foresee. And your focus will probably shift from positive to negative consequences. While it may be difficult to see what behavior will produce good results, it will be much easier to see what behavior will produce bad results. And so as a latter-day heir of Bentham and Mill you'll be more concerned with preventing pain and suffering than with promoting pleasure and enjoyment. And this will lead you to moral liberalism; which is to say, it will lead you to tolerate any behavior that does not produce pain. Instead of "maximize the happiness of mankind" being your guiding maxim, you will shift to "minimize the pain and suffering of mankind." This is what today's secularists have done.

Utilitarianism, in both its classical positive form (maximize mankind's pleasure) and its present-day negative form (minimize mankind's pain), bears a certain resemblance—a very superficial resemblance—to Catholic morality. It reminds us of the second of the two great commandments laid down by Jesus: "Thou shalt love the Lord thy God with all thy heart, and with all thy soul, and with all thy mind. This is the greatest and the first commandment. And the second is like unto it: Thou shalt love thy neighbor as thyself." (Matthew 22:37-39) However, despite the superficial resemblance, the Utilitarian commandments, both old and new, are in a number of ways a far cry from the Christian commandment:

- They have nothing to say about love of God.
- They do not make love of neighbor a kind of byproduct or corollary of love of God.
- They concern themselves with only the temporal/material well-being of others, not with their eternal/spiritual well-being.
- They define well-being in hedonistic terms, that is, it terms of pleasure and pain.
- They are not a summing-up of the rules of Christian morality; rather they are potential trumps for those rules. When Jesus said you must love your neighbor as yourself, he didn't mean that you were free to violate traditional rules against perjury, theft, adultery, murder, etc. if such violations would, in your opinion, prove helpful to your neighbor. But the Utilitarian rule says precisely this, at least by very clear implication.

Appendix II

A Feeling-based Morality

One last thing before I leave my discussion of secularist morality. Earlier I said that secularists are usually moral skeptics; they hold that there is no such thing as moral knowledge and that moral rules and values are nothing but man-made creations, creations of either society or the individual. But if so, how can we explain the very moralistic tendencies of many secularists? Typical secularists denounce certain things—e.g., war, racism, sexism, homophobia, capital punishment, female genital mutilation, denying equal rights to women, the burning of fossil fuels, voting for Republican candidates (the list goes on and on)—and denounce them with such vigor and in a spirit of such righteous indignation that they must feel certain that they are correct in their denunciations; they must feel certain that they are expressing in these denunciations something more than their mere personal likes and dislikes. But how can they feel certain about these moral judgments if they believe, as I have contended they do, that there is no such thing as moral knowledge? Don't you have to *know*, or at least think that you know, that X is wrong before you vehemently denounce somebody for doing X? Note that when secularists make these judgments they don't qualify them by saying "We Americans believe that X is wrong" or "I personally believe that X is wrong." No, they say simply, "X is wrong," and they appear to mean that it is wrong for all human beings regardless of what nation or culture or century these humans happen to belong to. How can moral skeptics say this? The answer is: They can say it by basing morality, not on that (to them) nonexistent thing, moral *knowledge*, but on that very clearly existent thing, moral *sentiment*. If there happens to be a sentiment or feeling held by all human beings, and if this sentiment is the basis of all human ideas about moral right and wrong, then it makes sense—at least it makes sense at first-glance—to condemn in an unqualified way behavior which offends this universal sentiment. Given this universal moral sentiment, the moral skeptic is just as entitled to make universal moral judgments as is the person who believes that there is a Natural Law of morality and that we humans are able to apprehend this Natural Law.

But *is* there such a universal sentiment or feeling? Yes, the secularist believes there is such a sentiment, *compassion*. We are made by nature in such a way that we resent it when undeserved harm is done to others. This is the theory of moral sentiment advanced about 250 years ago by Jean-Jacques Rousseau, often called the "father of Romanticism." Rousseau repudiated two widely held ideas current at his time: he repudiated both Calvin and Hobbes. First, he repudiated the Calvinist idea that humans are by nature wicked or depraved—a nature corrupted by the Fall of Adam and Eve. On the contrary, according to Rousseau, we humans are by nature good. If, in spite of this natural goodness, many humans are wicked, their wickedness is not natural to them; rather, it is a learned wickedness, something that has been instilled in them as a result of growing up and living in a morally corrupt society. Second, he repudiated the idea of Thomas Hobbes that humans are by nature 100 percent egoistic. Rousseau granted that we are often motivated by self-love, a natural sentiment; but this love of self, while it resembles egoism in some ways, and while it may be said that egoism is an exaggerated and perverted form of self-love, is something very different from egoism. Egoism makes every man the enemy of every other man; the egoist plays a zero-sum game against every other man. Rousseau denies that we are egoistic by nature. As long as an individual has his basic necessities met, and as long as he has not been corrupted by society, he is perfectly content that others should pursue their own happiness. And if self-love is our first sentiment, our second is compassion. It pains us to witness the pain and suffering of another human being. Thus it is natural for us to wish not to cause pain and suffering to others, and to wish to prevent others from causing such pain and suffering, and to wish to repair such pain and suffering when we can. And thus we feel guilty when we have caused such pain, and we feel indignant when we witness others causing such pain, and we feel a strong inclination to help relieve such pain. If self-love is the basis of our self-regarding morality, compassion is the basis of our other-regarding morality.

Our present-day moral liberal/secularist is, then, a Rousseauvian. We are by nature good, and this goodness includes the fundamental sentiment of compassion. We are compassionate animals, and if we act in a non-compassionate manner, we are acting abnormally, below the level of our nature; thus when we find somebody acting in a manner that is devoid of compassion we are entitled to denounce him/her as immoral. To be lacking in compassion is to be immoral, and to be immoral is to be lacking in compassion; for the moral liberal the two are synonymous expressions. To say that Smith is immoral is nothing other than to say he lacks compassion. If Smith does harm to Jones— whether physical, financial, reputational, or emotional harm—Smith does this because of a deficiency in compassion. But this is an acquired deficiency, not a natural deficiency; the evidence for this is that Smith, the wrongdoer himself, feels compassion for the victim of harm in situations in which Smith is not involved. If Smith, even though personally a bad man, sees a performance of "Othello," for instance, he feels sorry for Desdemona and blames Othello.

But is there any danger in basing a morality on feeling, not knowledge?— and in basing it on the feeling of compassion in particular? There are two questions here; let's take them one at a time. First, is it dangerous to base morality on feeling? Yes, for even granting (provisionally) for the sake of argument that a morality based on compassion would be a fine thing, there are feelings other than compassion that a morality might be based on, and some of these feelings, unlike compassion, can be very nasty. Nazism, to take a striking example, had a morality based on feelings—feelings such as anger and resentment and hatred and sadism. You don't have to be a Nazi to have a morality based on nasty feelings. Take, for example, a man whose complex of feelings leads him to beat up his girlfriend—but of course only, as he will assure us, "when she deserves it." Or take the racist whose *feelings* of aversion to blacks, Latinos, Jews, etc. leads him to actions harmful to members of those groups. The list of examples could go on and on. Of course the Rousseauvian would say that these are perverted emotions, not the fundamental emotions that nature has provided us with. To which the Nazi, the wife-beater, the racist, etc. would reply: "That's your opinion, Monsieur Rousseau; we have a different opinion."

Next, what about compassion itself? Granted, other emotions can be dangerous, but is there any danger in basing a morality on compassion? Yes, because a compassion-based morality depends heavily on the visual imagination of the compassionate person. Think of starving children in Africa. The abstract expression "starving children in Africa" evokes little in the way of compassion in most of us. But show us photos of those children with their blank looks, their distended bellies, their shrunken eyes with flies pestering them—then we feel compassion. X might be a much greater injustice than Y, but if I can easily picture Y and cannot easily picture X, my compassion will go to the person suffering Y and not to the person suffering X. For instance, for most persons it is much easier to picture and therefore feel sorry for a young woman who has an unwanted pregnancy than it is to picture and feel sorry for an unborn baby—a teeny-weeny little thing which is, practically speaking, invisible—who will be aborted to help the young woman out of her troubled situation. And so the compassionate person, feeling sorry for the young woman and not being able to feel sorry for the unborn baby, approves of the abortion— approves, that is, of something that moral knowledge, in contrast to the feeling of compassion, would say is homicide. Another example: there are millions of poor fatherless kids living in American urban ghettos, but if we don't *see* them—and most of us do not, because the mass media have little interest in showing us images of them,—then we don't find it easy to feel compassion for them. We are far more likely to feel compassion for a Hollywood movie star or a pop singer whose dog has died or whose boyfriend is cheating on her, because we see these movie stars and singers in magazines and on TV. Or take the twenty-six killings in late 2012 at the elementary school in Newtown,

Connecticut. Network television showed us horrifying images—of people running from the school, of anxious parents fearing the worst, of heart-broken parents whose worst fears came true, of friends and neighbors weeping, of the President of the United States barely able to control his feelings of sorrow, of funerals, and so on. And so we said to ourselves, and said with justice, "This is horrible, horrible, horrible." But in 2012 a vastly greater number of young blacks were killed in the ghettos of America. But network TV gave us relatively few images of them and their grieving families and their funerals. And so for the most part we yawn when we hear of these thousands of murders.

Made in the USA
San Bernardino, CA
29 January 2014